VERGIL
VOCABULARY CARDS
for AP Selections*

Dennis De Young

Bolchazy-Carducci Publishers, Inc.

Wauconda, Illinois USA

Editor
Laurie Haight Keenan

Cover Design
Adam Phillip Velez

Cover & Title Page Illustration
Thom Kapheim

Vergil Vocabulary Cards for AP˙ Selections

Dennis De Young

"Vergil's Meter" and "Glossary of Rhetorical Terms, Figures of Speech, and Metrical Devices" are by Barbara Weiden Boyd, from *Vergil's Aeneid: Selections from Books 1, 2, 4, 6, 10, and 12,* © copyright 2003, Bolchazy-Carducci Publishers, Inc.

Graphic Latin Grammar was prepared by James P. Humphreys, © copyright 2005, Bolchazy-Carducci Publishers, Inc., and is available in laminated cardstock from Bolchazy-Carducci Publisher, Inc.

© **2005 Bolchazy-Carducci Publishers, Inc.**

Bolchazy-Carducci Publishers, Inc.
1000 Brown Street
Wauconda, IL 60084 USA
www.bolchazy.com

Printed in the United States of America
2005
by United Graphics

ISBN-13: 978-0-86516-610-3
ISBN-10: 0-86516-610-2

ACKNOWLEDGEMENTS

I would like to thank the Davis Foundation and Montgomery Bell Academy for the grants and support for this book. Two of my Latin colleagues, Anne Christeson and Dr. Rick Seay, also helped proofread the text. I would like to dedicate this book to my mother and father, Thelma and Sidney De Young. They taught me everything I needed to know.

Dennis De Young

CATULLUS • CICERO • HORACE

AP*/IB/COLLEGE TITLES AND ANCILLARIES

WRITING PASSION: A Catullus Reader
Ronnie Ancona

Ancona's pedagogical and scholarly expertise has produced an outstanding Catullus reader that features the Latin text of 42 AP* poems with notes and vocabulary.

Student Text: xxxv + 261 pp. (2004) 6" x 9" Paperback, ISBN 0-86516-482-7
Teacher's Guide: vi + 122 pp. (2004) 8½" x 11" Paperback, ISBN 0-86516-483-5

CICERO THE PATRIOT
Cicero: Man, Politician, Writer, Orator
Student: ISBN 0-86516-587-4 • *Teacher:* ISBN 0-86516-588-2

HORACE: Selected Odes and Satire 1.9, 2nd edition
Ronnie Ancona

Ancona's edition includes the Latin text of all AP* poems with notes, same page and facing vocabulary.

Student Text: xxxiv + 174 pp. (1999, 2nd edition 2005) Paperback, ISBN 0-86516-608-0
Teacher's Guide: vi + 82 pp. (1999, 2nd edition 2005) Paperback, ISBN 0-86516-612-9

EMBERS OF THE ANCIENT FLAME, 2nd edition
Latin Love Poetry Selections from Catullus, Horace, and Ovid
Carol A. Murphy, Daniel G. Thiem, and Ryan T. Moore

This edition features the Latin text of 32 poems with facing-page grammar and vocabulary notes

xiv + 114 pp., (2001, 2nd edition 2005) Paperback, ISBN 0-86516-609-9

EXCELABILITY IN ADVANCED LATIN
A Workbook for Students
Applicable for all AP* authors
Student: ISBN 0-86516-512-2 • *Teacher:* ISBN 0-86516-518-1

THE KEY
Historical novel about Catullus
ISBN 0-86516-534-3

THE LOCK
Historical novel about Cicero
ISBN 0-86516-535-1

THE DOOR IN THE WALL
Historical novel about Caesar
ISBN 0-86516-533-5

CICERO'S PRO CAELIO, 3rd edition
Stephen Ciraolo

This newly revised edition provides all the linguistic and background material for the Cicero component of the AP* program in Latin literature. A terrific college text, too.

xxxi + 239 pp. (1997, 3rd edition 2003) 6" x 9" Paperback, ISBN 0-86516-559-9

HORACE SATIRE I.9: The Boor
Margaret A. Brucia and Madeleine M. Henry
This text includes the complete Latin text with notes on same and facing pages.

Student Text: Illus., 45 pp., (1998, Reprint 2000) Paperback, ISBN 0-86516-413-4
Teacher's Guide: 20 pp., (1998) Paperback, ISBN 0-86516-429-0

CATULLUS EXPANDED EDITION
Henry V. Bender and Phyllis Young Forsyth
Bender and Forsyth's edition includes all AP* Latin selections notes and vocabulary. A bonus non-AP* selection of poems is included.

Student Text: xii + 140 pp. (2005) Paperback, ISBN 0-86516-603-X
Teacher's Guide: 96 pp. (1996) Paperback, ISBN 0-86516-276-X
Teacher's Guide Supplement: vi + 42 pp. (2004) Paperback, ISBN 0-86516-576-9

OVID: Amores, Metamorphoses Selections
2nd edition
Charbra Adams Jestin and Phyllis B. Katz
This edition features the Latin AP* text with notes and translation questions and answers to guide comprehension outside of class.

Student Text: xx + 195 pp. (1999, Revised Reprint 2000)
Paperback, ISBN 0-86516-431-2
Teacher's Edition: viii + 72 pp. (1999, Revised Reprint, 2000)
Paperback, ISBN 0-86516-496-7

THE LIVING VOICE OF LATIN
Hear works of Cicero, Catullus, and Horace
Classical Latin: Order #23675 • *Classical Latin CD:* Order #SLT675
Vergil: Order #23685 • *Cicero:* Order #23680
Catullus/Horace: Order #23800

WHY HORACE? A Collection of Interpretations
20 essays plus bibliography
Paperback, ISBN 0-86516-417-7 • Hardbound, ISBN 0-86516-434-7

SCHOLA CANTANS
Cassette and Music Score, Modern music arrangements, Horace and Catullus selections
Cassette: 19 pp., ISBN 0-86516-357-X • *Music Score:* 46 pp., ISBN 0-86516-358-8
Cassette and Music Score Set: ISBN 0-86516-404-5

PERFORMING CICERO'S SPEECHES
An Experimental Workshop
VHS Videotape
ISBN 0-86516-488-6

HORACE FULLY PARSED WORD BY WORD
Every word parsed, Odes Books I & II
ISBN 0-86516-552-1

A SHORT GUIDE TO CLASSICAL MYTHOLOGY
Invaluable reference
ISBN 0-86516-309-X

COMPLETELY PARSED CICERO
The First Oration of Cicero Against Catiline
The Ultimate Resource for *In Catilinam I*
ISBN 0-86516-590-4

*AP is a registered trademark of the College Entrance Examination Board, which was not involved in the production of, and does not endorse, this product.

BOLCHAZY-CARDUCCI PUBLISHERS, INC.
www.BOLCHAZY.com

15+

ā, ab

15+

ac

15+

ad

15+

Aenéās, Aenéae, m.

15+

ágmen, -inis, n.

15+

áliquis, áliqua, áliquid

15+

álius, -a, -ud

15+

áltus, -a, -um

15+

ámor, -őris, m.

15+

ánimus, - ī, m.

and, and also;
as, than *(same as* átque*)*

from, away from; by *(+abl.)*

(ab-, *prefix;* aberrant, absent, abstain)

Aeneas *(son of Anchises)*

to, toward, near; at, by *(+acc.)*

(ad-, *prefix;* admonish)

someone, anyone

column, formation, rank, line; army

adj. - high, lofty; deep, profound
noun - the sea, heaven

(altitude)

another, other, else

soul, spirit, heart;
courage, daring, feeling

(animosity)

love, affection, fondness;
Cupid

(amorous)

15+

ánte

15+

ára, -ae, f.

15+

árma, -ṓrum, n. pl.

15+

árx, árcis, f.

15+

at

15+

átque

15+

aúra, -ae, f.

15+

aúrum, - ī, n.

15+

aut
aut...aut

15+

béllum, - ī, n.

altar

before, in front of *(+acc.);* previously

(antebellum)

citadel, fortress, stronghold; hill, peak

arms, weapons; tools, equipment

and, and also; as, than

but; yet, at least

gold

air, breeze, wind, blast; favor, light

war, combat, fight

(bellicose)

or
either...or

15+

caélum, -ī, n.

15+

cáput, cápitis, n.

15+

círcum

15+

clássis, clássis, f.

15+

cóniūnx, coniúgis, m. or f.

15+

córpus, -oris, n.

15+

cum

15+

cū́ra, -ae, f.

15+

dē

15+

déa, -ae, f.

head, the summit; life; person

(capital)

sky, heaven, the heavens; weather

(celestial)

fleet, division; ship

(class)

around, all around
at, near *(+ acc.)*

(circumnavigate)

body

(corporal)

spouse, husband, wife

(conjugal)

anxiety, distress, care, concern

(curator)

prep. - with *(+abl.)*
conj. - when, since, although

(com-, con-, *prefixes;* commit, connect)

goddess

(deity)

from, away from, down from;
concerning, according to *(+abl.)*

(de-, *prefix;* descend)

déus, déī, m.

déxter, déxtra, déxtrum

dícō, dícere, díxī, díctus

díctum, -ī, n.

Dídō, -ŏnis, f.

dívus, -a, -um

dō, dáre, dédī, dátus

dómus, -ūs, f.

dúcō, dúcere, dúxī, dúctus

dum

right, to the right; skillful;
favorable

(dexterity)

god, deity

(deify)

word, speech, command;
assertion, remark, saying

(diction, dictum, edict)

say, speak; sing; describe, name

(dictate, dictionary, contradict)

adj. - godlike, divine, of a deity
noun - god, goddess

(divine)

Dido *(queen of Carthage)*

house, home, dwelling, building;
family, race, line

(domestic)

give, appoint; grant, bestow;
emit, utter

(date, data)

while
until *(with subjunctive)*

lead, lead away, guide, conduct;
prolong; choose; think

(deduct, reduce)

ē, ex

égo

éō, íre, íī (ívī), ítus

et
et…et

fáma, -ae, f.

fátum, -ī, n.

férō, férre, túlī, látus

férrum, -ī, n.

flámma, -ae, f.

for, fárī, fátus

I

(egotistical)

out of, from; of; since;
according to *(+abl.)*

(ex-, e-, *prefixes;* exact, emit)

and, also, even, too;
both...and

(et cetera)

go, walk; ride; sail; move

(transition, initial)

fate; prediction

(fatal, fated)

report, rumor; saying;
talk; tradition

(famous, infamy)

iron; iron tool; sword; spear

(ferrous)

bring, carry, bear, wear;
report; offer; say

(transfer, refer, infer)

speak, say; prophesy

(infant)

flame, blaze; flame of passion

(inflammatory)

15+

gēns, géntis, f.

15+

hīc

15+

hic, haec, hoc

15+

hinc

15+

hóstis, hóstis, m. or f.

15+

iam

15+

ígnis, ígnis, m.

15+

ílle, ílla, íllud

15+

in

15+

íngēns, ingéntis

adv. - here

race, clan; descendant, offspring

(gentile, gentle)

from this place, hence;
on either side

this; the latter

(ad hoc)

now, at this time, already;
with a negative -longer, more

enemy, foe; stranger

(hostility)

that; he, she, it; the former

fire, light, lightning;
passion, fury, wrath

(ignition, igneous)

huge, vast, enormous;
extraordinary

in, on, upon, among *(+abl.)*
into, to; against *(+acc.)*

(in-, *prefix;* induct, initiate)

15+

ínter

15+

ípse, ípsa, ípsum

15+

Ītália, -ae, f.

15+

iúbeō, iubére, iússī, iússus

15+

Iū́nō, Iūnṓnis, f.

15+

lábor, -ṓris, m.

15+

lácrima, -ae, f.

15+

lắtus, -a, -um

15+

lī́men, -inis, n.

15+

lī́tus, -oris, n.

himself, herself, itself;
yourself; ourselves; myself

(ipso facto)

between, among, during *(+acc.)*

(inter-, *prefix;* interfere, intervene)

order, command; tell

(jussive)

Italy

labor, toil, exertion;
suffering, hardship

(laborious)

Juno
(wife of Jupiter, goddess of marriage)

broad, wide, extensive, spacious

(latitude)

tear, compassion

(lacrimation)

seashore, beach

(littoral)

threshold, door;
house, dwelling

(subliminal)

15+

lócus, -ī, m.

15+

lóngus, -a, -um
lóngē

15+

mágnus, -a, -um

15+

mánus, -ūs, f.

15+

médius, -a, -um

15+

méns, méntis, f.

15+

méus, -a, -um

15+

míser, mísera, míserum

15+

moénia, -ium, n. pl.

15+

múltus, -a, -um

adj. - long, extended
adv. (lóngē) - far off

(longitude, elongated)

place, spot; position

(location, locative)

ؤ

hand; band, troop; handiwork; deed

(manufacture, manuscript)

great, large, huge; mighty;
important

(magnitude, magnify)

mind, intellect; memory;
feeling; heart

(mental)

the middle of, middle

(mediator, medium)

wretched, miserable, sad, poor

(commiserate)

my, mine

much; many (pl.)
great, high; abundant

(multitude, multiple)

walls, ramparts; walled city;
structures

(munitions, ammunition)

nắtus, -a, -um

nē
-ne

nec
nec...nec

nōn

nóster, nóstra, nóstrum

nox, nóctis, f.

nunc

ō

óculus, -ī, m.

ómnis, ómnis, ómne

not; do not; lest;
Don't! *(with imperative)*
"*-ne*" *introduces a yes or no question*

adj. - born; made; destined, intended;
noun - a son

(prenatal, postnatal)

not, by no means

and...not, not;
neither...nor

night; death

(nocturnal)

our, ours

(nostrum, paternoster)

O! Oh!

now

all, every, whole

(omniscient, omnipotent)

eye

(ocular)

15+

ṓra, -ae, f.

15+

ṓrō, -ā́re, -ā́vī, -ā́tus

15+

ōs, ṓris, n.

15+

pars, pártis, f.

15+

páter, pátris, m.

15+

péctus, -oris, n.

15+

per

15+

pétō, pétere, petī́vī, petī́tus

15+

póssum, pósse, pótuī

15+

prémō, prémere, préssī, préssus

beg, plead; pray, beseech; speak

(orator)

shore, coast;
border, edge, rim

part, portion; side

(impartial, partition)

mouth; face; expression

(oral)

breast, chest, heart

(pectoral)

father, sire; ancestor

(patricide)

seek, aim at; attack; scan

(petition, compete)

through, along; throughout, during;
among; by means of *(+acc.)*

(per-, *prefix;* perfect)

press, pursue; overpower; bury,
conceal; restrain; control

(pressure, impress)

be able, can

(possible)

15+

Príamus, -ī, m.

15+

prímus, -a, -um

15+

-que
-que...-que

15+

quī, quae, quod

15+

quis, quid

15+

réferō, reférre, réttulī, relátus

15+

rēgína, -ae, f.

15+

régnum, -ī, n.

15+

rēs, réī (réī), f.

15+

rēx, régis, m.

first; chief, excellent (primary, prime)	Priam *(king of Troy)*
who, which; what; that (quibble, quorum)	and, also, even *(enclitic)* both...and
bring back; recall, speak, say (reference, relate)	who? what? which? why?
kingdom; royalty; realm, rule (reign)	queen (regulate)
king (regal)	thing, incident, matter; state; *pl.* - exploits, world (real, realistic, reality)

15+

sánguis, sánguinis, m.

15+

sē

15+

sed

15+

séquor, séquī, secútus sum

15+

sī

15+

sīc

15+

sócius, sóciī, m.

15+

sóror, -óris, f.

15+

stō, stắre, stétī, státus

15+

sub

himself, herself, itself;
themselves

(suicide, sui generis)

blood; bloodshed, slaughter;
descendant

(sanguine)

follow, pursue; accompany

(sequence)

but, moreover, however

thus, in this way

if, when, whether, in case that

sister

(sorority)

friend, comrade, ally

(social, society)

under, beneath, at the foot of *(+abl.)*
to, toward, up to *(+acc.)*

(sub-, *prefix;* subterranean)

stand; be built; linger, remain

(stance)

15+

sum, ésse, fúī, futūrus

15+

súmmus, -a, -um

15+

súus, -a, -um

15+

tális, tális, tále

15+

tándem

15+

tántus, -a, -um

15+

téctum, -ī, n.

15+

télum, -ī, n.

15+

téneō, tenḗre, ténuī, téntus

15+

térra, -ae, f.

highest, uppermost;
loftiest, supreme

(summit, summary)

be, exist

(essence, essential)

such, of such a kind;
the following

his, her, its, their *(the subject's)*

so great, so much, so far

(tantamount)

finally, at last; pray now

spear, shaft, javelin; weapon

roof; house, dwelling

earth, land; soil

(terrain)

hold, keep, have; occupy;
hold back, detain; reach

(tenacious)

15+

Teúcrī, - ṓrum, m. pl.

15+

tot

15+

tṓtus, -a, -um

15+

Trṓia, -ae, f.

15+

tū

15+

tum

15+

Túrnus, -ī, m.

15+

túus, -a, -um

15+

úbi

15+

úmbra, -ae, f.

so many, such a number of;
as many

Trojans

Troy

all, entire, whole

(totalitarian)

then, at that time, in those times;
further

you *(sing.)*

your *(sing.)*

Turnus *(leader of the Rutulians)*

shadow, shade, ghost

(umbrage, umbrella)

where; when

(ubiquitous)

15+

únda, -ae, f.

15+

űnus, -a, -um

15+

úrbs, úrbis, f.

15+

ut

15+

-ve

15+

véniō, veníre, vḗnī, véntus

15+

véntus, -ī, m.

15+

vía, víae, f.

15+

vídeō, vidḗre, vī́dī, vī́sus

15+

vir, vírī, m.

one; only, alone

(unity, union)

wave; water, sea

(undulation)

as; when; so that; how!

city

(suburb)

come, arrive; go

(venue, convene)

or *(enclitic)*

way, road, path;
method, mode

(viaduct)

wind

(ventilation)

man, male

(virile)

see, perceive; understand;
seem, appear *(passive)*

(visible)

15+

vīs, vīs, f.

15+

vócō, vocǻre, vocǻvī, vocǻtus

15+

vólvō, vólvere, vólvī, volútus

15+

vōx, vócis, f.

15+

vúlnus, vúlneris, n.

9–14

Achíllēs, -is, m.

9–14

aéquor, -oris, n.

9–14

aéquus, -a, -um

9–14

ágō, ágere, ḗgī, ǻctus

9–14

áit

call, name; address;
invite; invoke

(vocation, vocative)

force, violence;
pl. - strength

(violent)

voice; cry, call; word, saying

(vocal)

turn, roll; ordain, decree; glide;
ponder, consider

(revolve, involve)

Achilles, *(greatest of the Greek
fighters at Troy)*

wound, injury, deadly blow

(invulnerable)

even, level; just, fair

(equal, inequity)

sea, surface of the sea;
waves; plain

says, asserts

do; drive; pursue; conduct
come! *(imperative)*

(action, active)

9–14

árdeō, ardḗre, ársī, arsū́rus

9–14

árvum, -ī, n.

9–14

áter, átra, átrum

9–14

aúdeō, audḗre, aúsus sum

9–14

aúdiō, audī́re, audī́vī, audī́tus

9–14

āvértō, āvértere, āvértī, āvérsus

9–14

bis

9–14

cápio, cápere, cḗpī, cáptus

9–14

cắsus, -ūs, m.

9–14

caúsa, -ae, f.

plowed land, cultivated field; field

burn, be on fire, blaze

(ardent, arson)

dare, venture, risk, be eager

(audacious, audacity)

black, dark, sable;
dusky, gloomy; deadly

turn away, avert, remove

(averse)

hear, listen to

(audible, audience)

seize, grasp, capture; form;
captivate, deceive

(captive, caption)

twice, double

(bisexual)

cause, reason, motive

(causation)

chance; fall; ruin, failure

(casualty)

cávus, -a, -um

céntum

cérnō, cérnere, crḗvī, crḗtus

cíngō, cíngere, cínxī, cínctus

clámor, -ṓris, m.

cómes, cómitis, m. or f.

cóndō, cóndere, cóndidī, cónditus

cóntrā

corrípiō, corrípere, corrípuī, corréptus

crḗdō, crḗdere, crḗdidī, crḗditus

one hundred

(century, centurion)

hollow, excavated

(excavate)

equip, gird oneself;
surround, encircle

(succinct)

discern, perceive, distinguish;
separate; decide

(concern)

friend, companion, comrade

shout, roar; applause

(clamor, exclaim)

against; opposite, facing *(+acc.)*

(contra-, *prefix;* contradict)

found, establish, build; bury

(condiment, abscond)

believe, trust, confide in *(+dat.)*

(credence, incredible)

seize, snatch, grasp;
attack

crūdḗlis, crūdḗlis, crūdḗle

cúrsus, -ūs, m.

Dánaus, -ī, m.

díēs, diḗī, m.

dólor, -ṓris, m.

dṓnum, -ī, n.

dúlcis, dúlcis, dúlce

dū́rus, -a, -um

énim

équidem

running, a run, running course;
journey; haste

(course)

cruel, unfeeling, hard, pitiless

(cruelty)

day

(diary, meridian)

of Danaus *(a famous Greek king)*
pl. the Greeks

gift, present

(donor)

pain, suffering, anguish,
distress, grief, trouble

(dolorous)

hard, harsh, vigorous;
pitiless, unyielding

(endure, durable)

sweet, agreeable, delightful

(dulcimer)

indeed, truly

for, namely, that is to say

équus, - ī, m.

ērípiō, ērípere, ērípuī, ēréptus

érrō, -áre, -ávī, -átus

étiam

extrémus, -a, -um

fáciō, fácere, fḗcī, fáctus

fī́nis, fī́nis, m.

flúctus, -ūs, m.

fórs, fórtis, f.

fórtis, fórtis, fórte

rescue, deliver, free; tear out, wrest, pluck, tear	horse (equine)
also, too, even; still	wander, stray, roam; be in error (errant, aberrant)
make, do; produce, build; grant, offer; suppose (factory, manufacture)	outermost, utmost, farthest; final; tip of; edge of (extremities)
wave, tide, billow; surge (fluctuate)	end, boundary, limit; goal; *pl.* - territory (finite, infinite)
brave, strong, courageous (fortitude)	chance, luck, fortune (fortuitous)

fortūna, -ae, f.

fúga, -ae, f.

fúgiō, fúgere, fūgī, fúgitus

fúndō, fúndere, fūdī, fūsus

fúrō, fúrere

fúrōr, -ṓris, m.

gémitus, -ūs, m.

génitor, -ṓris, m.

génus, géneris, n.

grávis, grávis, gráve

flight, rapid movement

(fugue)

fortune, chance, luck

(fortunate)

pour, pour out, shed;
spread; extend

(effusive)

flee, run away, escape

(fugitive)

rage, madness, fury; passion

(furor)

rage, rave, be out of one's mind

father

groan, sighing, complaint

heavy, weighty; serious, burdened;
full of

(gravity)

race, stock, family;
birth, noble birth; descendant

(generation, genus)

haud

heu

hómō, hóminis, m.

iáctō, -áre, ávī, -átus

ídem, eádem, ídem

imágō, imáginis, f.

immánis, immánis, immáne

impérium, impériī, n.

ímus, -a, -um

incípiō, incípere, incépī, incéptus

alas!

not, not at all, by no means

throw out; consider, discuss; boast;
pronounce, utter, speak

person, human being, man

(homicide, homo sapiens)

image; ghost, vision; reminder

(imagination)

the same

(identity)

supreme power, sovereignty
command, order

(imperial, imperious)

huge; monstrous, frightful

begin

(inception, conception)

lowest, deepest, the bottom of;
last

īnstō, īnstā́re, ī́nstitī

intéreā

Iúppiter, Ióvis, m.

íra, írae, f.

iúngō, iúngere, iúnxī, iū́nctus

laétus, -a, -um

Látium, Látiī, n.

légō, légere, lḗgī, lḗctus

lū́men, lū́minis, n.

málus, -a, -um

meanwhile

pursue, press;
stand on, take a position

(instant)

anger, fury, hatred

Jupiter *(husband and brother of Juno)*

(irate)

happy, delighted, joyous;
pleasant, grateful; fertile

join, unite, connect

(junction)

survey; gather, collect, choose;
read

Latium *(a district in Italy
south of the Tiber)*

(lecture, legible)

evil, bad, wicked; hostile

light; *pl.* - eyes

(malevolent, malicious)

(luminous)

9–14

máneō, manḗre, mā́nsī, mā́nsus

9–14

máre, máris, n.

9–14

métus, -ūs, m.

9–14

mísceō, miscḗre, míscuī, míxtus

9–14

míttō, míttere, mī́sī, míssus

9–14

mōns, móntis, m.

9–14

mórior, mórī, mórtuus sum

9–14

mors, mórtis, f.

9–14

mū́rus, mū́rī, m.

9–14

namque

sea

(marine, maritime)

remain, stay; await

(immanent, mansion)

mix, mingle, intermingle;
confuse

(mixture)

fear, dread, apprehension

(meticulous)

mountain, hill; mass, heap

(paramount, tantamount)

send, let go; throw; dismiss

(emit, mission)

death, destruction, ruin

(mortal)

die, expire; decay, wither

(mortuary)

for

wall, city wall

(mural, immure)

9–14

nắvis, nắvis, f.

9–14

néque
néque...néque

9–14

nőmen, nőminis, n.

9–14

nōs

9–14

nőtus, -a, -um

9–14

nóvus, -a, -um

9–14

nűbēs, nűbis, m. or f.

9–14

nűmen, nűminis, n.

9–14

ópus, óperis, n.

9–14

órbis, órbis, m.

and...not; also...not;
neither...nor

ship

(navy, naval)

we, us

name, title; fame

(nominate)

new, young, fresh; novel

(novice, renovate)

known, famous; customary

(noted)

divine power, divinity;
god, goddess

(numinous)

cloud, mist, vapor

circle; world; shield; coil

(orb, orbit)

work, handiwork, labor, toil;
structure; artistic work

(opera)

Pállās, Pallántis, m.

párēns, paréntis, m. or f.

párō, -áre, -ávī, -átus

pélagus, -ī, n.

pőnō, pőnere, pósuī, pósitus

pópulus, -ī, m.

pórta, -ae, f.

prō

púer, púerī, m.

púlcher, púlchra, púlchrum

parent, ancestor

(parental)

Pallas *(son of Evander,
killed by Turnus)*

sea

(pelagic)

prepare, arrange, make ready

(compare, repair)

people, nation, crowd

(populace, population)

put, place; establish;
lay aside; bury

(position, deposit)

for; before; on account of;
instead of *(+abl.)*

(pro-, *prefix;* proactive)

door, gate; entrance; outlet

(portal)

beautiful, handsome, noble

(pulchritude)

boy

(puerile)

púppis, púppis, f.

quaérō, quaérere, quaesívī, quaesítus

quális, quális, quále

quam

rápiō, rápere, rápuī, ráptus

réddō, réddere, réddidī, rédditus

relínquō, relínquere, relíquī, relíctus

Rōmắnus, -a, -um

rúō, rúere, rúī, ruitúrus

sácer, sácra, sácrum

seek, look for, ask for

(inquiry)

stern, poop deck; ship

(poop)

how, how much; than; as

what sort?; of such a kind, such as

(quality)

give back, restore;
reply, answer

(rendition)

seize, snatch, tear, pluck; drive;
ravish, whirl

(rapture, rapt)

Roman

leave behind, abandon, relinquish

(relic, derelict)

holy, sacred;
n. pl. - sacrifice

(sacrament)

rush, hurry; fall down, tumble, crash;
plow

(ruin)

saévus, -a, -um

sáxum, -ī, n.

scópulus, -ī, m.

sḗdēs, sḗdis, f.

sḗsē

sídus, síderis, n.

sílva, -ae, f.

sṓlus, -a, -um

sómnus, -ī, m.

sors, sórtis, f.

large stone, boulder; rock

(saxicolous)

savage, fierce, ferocious;
terrible

seat, dwelling-place; foundation

(sediment)

cliff, crag, ledge; rock

constellation, group of stars;
the sky, heaven; weather

(consider, desire)

himself, herself, itself, themselves;
(intensive form of sē)

alone, only, sole; single

(solitary)

woods, forest

(sylvan, Pennsylvania)

luck, lot; fate, prophecy, destiny

(consort)

sleep, slumber

(somniferous, insomnia)

spēs, spéī, f.

spólium, spóliī, n.

súbeō, subíre, subívī, súbitus

súper

súpplex, súpplicis *(adj. or noun)*

súrgō, súrgere, surrḗxī, surrḗctus

támen

tántum

téllūs, tellū́ris, n.

témplum, -ī, n.

pl. - arms stripped from an enemy, booty; prize

(spoils)

hope, expectation

(despair)

above, over, on top of; concerning, about *(+abl.)*

(super-, *prefix;* superstructure)

advance, approach; enter; support; go under; arise

rise, get up, stand up; ascend

(surge, insurgency)

suppliant; beseeching, entreating

(supplicate)

so much, so greatly; only

however, nevertheless, still

temple, sanctuary, shrine

(templar)

earth, ground, land; globe

(tellurian)

témpus, -oris, n.

téndō, téndere, teténdī, téntus

térgum, -ī, n.

tóllō, tóllere, sústulī, sublátus

Trōiánus, -a, -um

túrbo, -áre, -ávī, -átus

Týrius, -a, -um

úllus, -a, -um

úmerus, -ī, m.

únā

stretch, extend; present;
aim; exert, strive

(tend, pretend)

time; occasion, opportunity

(temporaray, temporal)

lift, raise; erect; extol, exalt;
remove, destroy

(extol)

back, rear; hide, leather; rear

(tergite)

disturb, make an uproar; trouble

(turbine, turbid)

Trojan

any, any one

Tyrian, Carthaginian

at once, together, at the same time

shoulder, upper arm

(humerus)

9–14

vătēs, vătis, m. or f.

9–14

Vénus, Véneris, f.

9–14

vértex, vérticis, m.

9–14

vértō, vértere, vértī, vérsus

9–14

vĕrus, -a, -um

9–14

víncō, víncere, vícī, víctus

9–14

vólō, -ăre, -ăvī, -ătus

9–14

vólō, vélle, vóluī

9–14

vúltus, -ūs, m.

5–8

accéndō, accéndere, accéndī, accénsus

Venus *(goddess of love;*
Aeneas's mother)

(venereal)

seer, prophet, prophetess

(vatic)

turn, direct, change;
twist; destroy

(convert, version)

whirlpool, vortex; peak, summit

(vertical)

conquer, overcome, defeat;
banish

(invincible, victory)

true; real, actual; genuine

(verify, verity)

wish, want, desire

(volition)

fly

(volatile)

inflame, set on fire;
arouse, inspire

face; appearance, expression

accípiō, accípere, accḗpī, accéptus

ā́cer, ā́cris, ā́cre

Achā́tēs, Achā́tae, m.

ā́deō, adī́re, adī́vī, ā́ditus

ā́deō

ā́dfor, adfā́rī, adfā́tus sum

ā́dloquor, ā́dloquī, adlocū́tus sum

ā́dsum, adésse, ā́dfuī, adfutū́rus

advérsus, -a, -um

aéger, aégra, aégrum

sharp, keen, fierce, violent

(acrid, acrimonious)

receive, accept; welcome, admit;
learn, hear, conceive

(acceptance)

approach, go to; reach, visit,
encounter, meet

Achates *(Aeneas's frequent companion)*

address, speak to

(affable)

so, to that degree, so much

be present, be at hand, be near;
assist

address, speak to; accost

sick, diseased; weary, weak

turned toward, opposing, facing;
averse

(adversity)

5–8

Aéolus, -ī, m.

5–8

áēr, áeris, m.

5–88

aetérnus, -a, -um

5–8

aéthēr, aétheris, m.

5–8

agnóscō, agnóscere, agnṓvī, ágnitus

5–8

ála, álae, f.

5–8

álter, áltera, álterum

5–8

amícus, -a, -um

5–8

āmíttō, āmíttere, āmísī, āmíssus

5–8

ámō, -áre, -ávī, -átus

air, breeze, mist, cloud, fog

(aerate)

Aeolus *(god of the winds)*

upper air, heaven, sky

(ether, ethereal)

eternal, everlasting

(eternity)

wing, pinion;
group of hunters

recognize

adj. - friendly
noun - friend

(amicable)

one of two, the other, a second

(alternative)

love, cherish, like

(amorous, paramour)

lose, send away; let go

ampléctor, ampléctī, ampléxus sum

an
an…an

Anchísēs, Anchísae, m.

ánima, -ae, f.

Ánna, -ae, f.

ánnus, -ī, m.

antíquus, -a, -um

ántrum, -ī, n.

apériō, aperíre, apéruī, apértus

Apóllō, Apóllinis, m.

whether
whether...or

enfold, embrace, wind about

breath; life, existence;
soul, spirit

(animated)

Anchises *(Aeneas's father)*

year; season

(annual, annuity)

Anna *(Dido's sister)*

cave, cavern, grotto

ancient, aged, former

(antiquity)

Apollo*(god of prophecy and music)*

open, uncover, disclose, reveal

(aperture)

appắreō, appārḗre, appắruī, appắritus

árbor, -oris, f.

ártus, -ūs, m.

Ascánius, Ascániī, m.

aspíciō, aspícere, aspéxī, aspéctus

attóllō, attóllere

aúreus, -a, -um

aúris, aúris, f.

Ausónius, -a, -um

bónus, -a, -um

tree, trunk, shoot

(arboreal)

appear, be disclosed, be seen

(apparition)

Ascanius *(Aeneas's son)*

joint, limb; frame, body

lift up, raise; rear

look at, look upon, behold;
regard

(aspect)

ear

(aural)

golden, of gold

(aureole)

good, kind, useful

(bona fide, bonanza)

Ausonian, Italian

5–8

cádō, cádere, cécidī, cắsus

5–8

caécus, -a, -um

5–8

caédēs, caédis, f.

5–8

cámpus, -ī, m.

5–8

cánō, cánere, cécinī, cántus

5–8

cắrus, -a, -um

5–8

cḗdō, cḗdere, céssī, céssus

5–8

céler, céleris, célere

5–8

cértus, -a, -um

5–8

cérvīx, cervícis, f.

blind; dark; hidden

(caecilian)

fall, fall down, descend;
fail, sink, die

(cadence)

field, plain, level place

(camp, campus)

killing, slaughter, murder

dear, precious, valued

(caress, charity)

sing, sound; play

(canticle)

quick, swift, speedy

(accelerate, celerity)

go from, remove, withdraw, abandon

(recess)

neck, nape

(cervical)

determined, resolved, fixed, certain

(certify, certitude)

circúmdō, circúmdare, circúmdedī, circúmdatus

claúdō, claúdere, claúsī, claúsus

clípeus, clípeī, m.

cṓgō, cṓgere, coḗgī, coáctus

cólligō, collígere, collḗgī, colléctus

cóma, -ae, f.

cómitor, comitā́rī, comitā́tus sum

compṓnō, compṓnere, compósuī, compósitus

cōnū́bium, conū́bīī, n.

cor, córdis, n.

shut, enclose, close

(clause, closet)

surround, place around, encompass

collect; compel, force; urge

(cogent)

shield, round shield, buckler

hair; foliage

(comet)

gather, collect; assemble

(collective)

collect, lay; put to rest, quiet

(composed, composition)

accompany, attend, follow

heart, spirit, feelings

(cordial)

marriage

(connubial)

Creúsa, -ae, f.

crī́nis, crī́nis, m. or f.

cruéntus, -a, -um

cúnctor, cunctā́rī, cunctā́tus sum

cúrrus, -ūs, m.

Dardánius, -a, -um

dēmíttō, dēmíttere, dēmī́sī, dēmíssus

dḗserō, dēsérere, dēséruī, dēsértus

dī́rus, -a, -um

dī́ves, dī́vitis

hair

(crinoline)

Creusa *(Aeneas's wife)*

delay, linger, hesitate

bloody, stained, spotted with blood;
cruel

Trojan, of Dardanus

chariot, car, wagon

leave, forsake, abandon, desert

(deserter)

let down, drop, let fall, shed;
derive

rich, wealthy, opulent

(Dives)

ominous, fearful, awful,
dreadful, horrible

(dire)

5–8

dóceō, docḗre, dócuī, dóctus

5–8

dux, dúcis, m.

5–8

ecce

5–8

éfferō, efférre, éxtulī, ēlā́tus

5–8

éffor, effā́rī, effā́tus sum

5–8

ēgrégius, -a, -um

5–8

énsis, énsis, m.

5–8

érgō

5–8

Eúrus, -ī, m.

5–8

exánimus, -a, -um

leader, guide; general

(ductile)

teach, instruct, inform

(docent)

carry out, take away;
bear, produce

(elated)

behold! look!

distinguished, excellent, eminent

(egregious)

utter, tell, speak out, say

(ineffable)

therefore, consequently, accordingly

sword

lifeless, dead

(exanimate)

Eurus *(a southeast or east wind)*

excípiō, excípere, excḗpī, excéptus

exúviae, -ā́rum, f.

fácilis, fácilis, fácile

fállō, fállere, feféllī, fálsus

fās, n.

fídēs, fidḗī, f.

fī́dus, -a, -um

fī́gō, fī́gere, fī́xī, fī́xus

foédō, -ā́re, -ā́vī, -ā́tus

fórma, -ae, f.

spoils; relics; skin

(exuviation)

take out, withdraw;
take up, catch, receive

(exception)

trip, fall; err, make a mistake,
deceive oneself; escape the notice

(infallible)

easy

(facilitate, facilities)

faith, loyalty, belief, reliance;
trustworthiness

(fidelity, fiduciary)

divine law;
(with est) it is lawful

fix, fasten; pierce

(affix)

loyal, faithful, credible

(fidelity)

form, shape; beauty

(format)

make foul, defile, pollute;
mar, mangle, disfigure

fóveō, fovére, fṓvī, fṓtus

fráter, frátris, m.

frémō, frémere, frémuī, frémitus

frústrā

fúlgeō, fulgére, fúlsī

fū́nus, fū́neris, n.

géminus, -a, -um

gérō, gérere, géssī, géstus

Graíus, -a, -um

hábeō, habḗre, hábuī, hábitus

brother

(fraternal, fraternity)

cherish, fondle, caress

in vain, for nothing

(frustration)

roar, resound, howl; applaud;
grumble

(fremitus)

funeral procession, funeral rites, burial;
death, murder

(funereal)

flash, glitter, gleam, shine

(fulgent)

bear, carry, wage; wear

(gestation)

twin, double, two

(Gemini)

have, hold, support, carry;
consider, regard

(habit, habitual)

Greek

haéreō, haerére, haésī, haésus

hásta, -ae, f.

Héctor, -oris, m.

hḗrōs, herṓös, m.

híems, híemis, f.

hónor, -ṓris, m.

hūc

iáceō, iacḗre, iácuī, iácitus

Īlíacus, -a, -um

impéllō, impéllere, ímpulī, impúlsus

spear, lance, javelin

(hastate)

cling, stick, be fastened;
linger, pause

(adhesive, inherent)

hero, demigod

(heroic)

Hector *(Troy's champion, son of Priam)*

honor, repute, esteem, distinction;
offering; charm

(dishonor)

winter, winter time; storm

(hiemal)

lie, be prostrate, lie at rest

(adjacent)

here, to this place, hither;
to this point, so far

strike against, strike, push;
set in motion

(impulsive)

of Ilium, Trojan

impṓnō, impṓnere, impósuī, impósitus

inā́nis, inā́nis, inā́ne

incéndō, incéndere, incéndī, incénsus

incúmbō, incúmbere, incúbuī, incúbitus

īnfélīx, īnfēlī́cis

ingrédior, íngredī, ingréssus sum

inimī́cus, -a, -um

ínquit

īnséquor, īnséquī, īnsecū́tus sum

īnsígnis, īnsígnis, īnsígne

useless, empty, meaningless

(inane)

place upon, put on

(impose, impostor)

lean, press; bend to, oppress;
brood over

(incumbent)

set fire to, burn; rouse, incite

(incensed)

advance, go forward; undertake

(ingress)

unfortunate, unlucky, miserable;
barren

(infelicitous)

says, said

hostile, unfriendly, hateful;
damaging

(inimical)

distinguished, remarkable, prominent

(ensign, insignia)

follow after, come next;
proceed, go on

is, éa, id

íste, ísta, ístud

íterum

Iúlus, -ī, m.

Iúppiter, Ióvis, m.

iūs, iúris, n.

iúvenis, iúvenis, iúvene

iúvō, iuvắre, iúvī, iútus

Karthágō, Kartháginis, f.

lắbor, lắbī, lápsus sum

that *(of yours)*
(often contempuous)

he, she, it; this, that

Iulus *(another name for Ascanius, Aeneas's son)*

again, a second time, once more

(reiterate)

right, justice, duty

(jury)

Jupiter *(chief god of the Romans)*

help, aid, assist, serve; delight

(adjutant, adjuvant)

adj. - young, youthful;
noun - young person

(juvenile)

slip, glide, slide, move; sink, fall

(elapse, lapse)

Carthage *(Dido's city)*

létum, -ī, n.

lēx, légis, f.

Líbya, -ae, f.

Líbycus, -a, -um

línquō, línquere, líquī

lócō, -áre, -ávī, -átus

lóquor, lóquī, locútus sum

lúcus, -ī, m.

lústrō, -áre, -ávī, -átus

lūx, lúcis, f.

law, precept, regulation, principle

(legal, legislature)

death, annihilation

(lethal)

Libyan, of Libya

Libya *(region of northern Africa)*

place, put, lay; establish

(location, locative)

go away, leave, depart from, abandon

(relinquish)

sacred grove, wood

speak, talk, say, tell; declare

(loquacious)

light, brightness; day; life
pl. - heavenly bodies

(lucent)

review, observe, examine;
illuminate; purify; traverse

(luster, illustration)

maéstus, -a, -um

mágis

mā́nēs, -ium, m. pl.

mā́ter, mā́tris, f.

mémini, meminísse

mémor, mémoris

mémorō, -ā́re, -ā́vī, -ā́tus

mī́ror, mīrā́rī, mīrā́tus sum

míseror, miserā́rī, miserā́tus sum

módus, -ī, m.

more, rather

sorrowful, dejected, despondent

mother; native land

(maternal)

departed spirit, ghost, shade

mindful, remembering

(memory, memorabilia)

remember, recollect

wonder, marvel at, be astonished

(miraculous)

mention, recount, speak of, tell

(memorable)

measure; way, manner; method

(mode, module)

lament, commiserate; pity

(commiserate)

mṓlēs, mōlis, f.

mṓlior, mōlī́rī, mōlī́tus sum

móllis, móllis, mólle

mónstrō, -ā́re, -ā́vī, -ā́tus

móra, -ae, f.

móror, morā́rī, morā́tus sum

mortā́lis, mortā́lis, mortā́le

mōs, mṓris, m.

móveō, movḗre, mṓvī, mṓtus

mū́nus, mū́neris, n.

exert, strive, toil;
build; rouse

mass, weight; greatness;
difficulty, labor, trouble

(mole)

point out, exhibit, indicate, inform;
urge, advise

(monstrance)

soft, yielding, tender, gentle

(emollient, mollify)

delay, stay, remain, linger

(moratorium)

delay, procrastination;
obstruction, hindrance

practice, custom, habit; institution

(mores)

mortal, transient

(immortal)

service, office; burial

(remunerate)

move, remove, shake;
excite, arouse, agitate

(motion, immovable)

5–8

múrmur, múrmuris, n.

5–8

nam

5–8

némus, némoris, n.

5–8

nēquíquam

5–8

nũllus, -a, -um

5–8

nýmpha, -ae, f.

5–8

obscũrus, -a, -um

5–8

Olýmpus, -ī, m.

5–8

omnípotēns, omnipoténtis

5–8

ops, ópis, f.

for	murmur, roar, growling, grumbling, crash
in vain, without reason	wood, grove, forest
nymph	no, none; worthless; no one (nullify)
Mt. Olympus *(home of the gods)*	dark, shady, obscure; unknown (obscurity)
aid, help, assistance; means, wealth, resources	almighty, omnipotent

óptō, -ā́re, -ā́vī, -ā́tus

óstium, óstiī, n.

pándō, pándere, pándī, pássus

pār, páris

párvus, -a, -um

páteō, patḗre, pátuī

pátior, pátī, pássus sum

pátria, -ae, f.

pátrius, -a, -um

pāx, pā́cis, f.

door; mouth, entrance; harbor

(ostiole)

choose, prefer; hope for

(option)

equal, even; well-balanced

(parity)

spread out, extend; open, lay open

(expansive)

be open, stand open

(patent)

small; short, brief

native land, own country; home

(patriotic)

bear, support, suffer, endure; allow

(patient, passive)

peace, reconciliation

(pacifist)

fatherly; traditional

Penā́tēs, Penā́tium, m. pl.

péndeō, pendḗre, pepéndī

pénitus, -a, -um

Pérgama, -ṓrum, n. pl.

pérgō, pérgere, perrḗxī, perréctus

pēs, pédis, m.

Phoébus, -ī́, m.

Phrýgius, -a, -um

píetās, pietā́tis, f.

píus, -a, -um

hang, be suspended; loiter

(pendant)

household gods, gods of the state

Troy

inwardly, deeply; thoroughly;
far within

foot; sheet *(nautical term)*

(pedal, pedestal)

proceed, go on, hasten

Phrygian, Tyrian

Apollo *(god of prophecy and music)*

devoted, dutiful, devout,
conscientious

(impiety)

devotion, loyalty, dutiful conduct;
sense of duty

(impious)

poéna, -ae, f.

póntus, -ī, m.

pórtus, -ūs, m.

póscō, póscere, popóscī

post

póstquam

précor, precắrī, precắtus sum

príor, príor, príus

prócul

prốlēs, prốlis, f.

sea, waves

penalty, punishment

(subpoena)

ask, beg, request; demand,

port, harbor

after, when

after, behind *(+acc.);*
afterwards

(postpone)

former, previous, prior, first

(priority)

ask, beg, entreat, request;
invoke

(imprecate)

offspring, children, descendants

(prolific)

in the distance, far, from afar

púgna, -ae, f.

Pýrrhus, -ī, m.

quā

quándō

quīn

quísquis, quídquid

quō

quóndam

quóque

rápidus, -a, -um

Pyrrhus *(Achilles' son)*

fight, battle

(pugnacious)

when; since; if...ever

where? how? in any way

whoever, whatever; everyone who

why not? but, indeed

once, at some time, at one time;
sometimes

where; at which time

fierce; rushing, swift

also, too

(rapidity)

5–8

recípiō, recípere, recḗpī, recéptus

5–8

redū́cō, redū́cere, redū́xī, reductus

5–8

rḗgius, -a, -um

5–8

rḗgō, régere, rḗxī, rḗctus

5–8

remíttō, remíttere, remī́sī, remíssus

5–8

repṓnō, repṓnere, repósuī, repósitus

5–8

respíciō, respícere, respéxī, respéctus

5–8

revī́sō, revī́sere

5–8

rṓbur, rṓboris, n.

5–8

Rútulī, -ṓrum, m. pl.

lead back, bring back

(reduction)

receive, take back; recover, rescue

(recipient, receptacle)

rule, control; direct, guide

(regent)

royal, regal, kingly

put back, restore; stretch out;
lay aside, store

(repository)

send back, drive back;
loosen, relax; give up

(remission)

look back; revisit

(revise)

look back, gaze at, look for

(respect)

Rutulians *(Turnus's tribe)*

hardwood, oak; tree trunk; oak tree;
strength

(robust)

sácrō, -ā́re, -ā́vī, -ā́tus

sécō, secā́re, sécuī, séctus

sédeō, sedḗre, sḗdī, séssus

séptem

sérmō, sermṓnis, m.

sérvō, -ā́re, -ā́vī, -ā́tus

seu

Sibýlla, -ae, f.

símul

síne

cut, reap, carve; operate, divide

(sect, sector)

consecrate, dedicate, devote

(sacrament)

seven

(September)

sit; hold court

(session, sedentary)

save, guard, keep; watch

(conservative)

speech, conversation;
talk, report, rumor

(sermon)

the Sibyl *(prophetess of Apollo)*

whether; or if

without *(+abl.)*

(sinecure)

at the same time, simultaneously

sínō, sínere, sī́vī, sítus

sínus, -ūs, m.

sī́ve

sólum, -ī, n.

sólvō, sólvere, sólvī, solū́tus

sónō, sonā́re, sónuī, soní́tus

spḗrō, -ā́re, -ā́vī, ā́tus

spū́mō, -ā́re, -ā́vī, -ā́tus

stérnō, stérnere, strā́vī, strā́tus

strídeō, strīdḗre, strī́dī

bay; fold; bosom

(insinuate)

allow, permit; desert

whether; or if

ground, base, foundation

(soil)

resound, make a noise;
speak, express

(sonar, sonic)

loosen, relax; release, unfurl;
dispel, dismiss

(resolve, dissolve)

foam, froth, spray

(spume)

hope, look for, expect

(despair)

make a harsh noise, hiss;
grate, creak

(strident)

spread out; overthrow, level, flatten

(stratum)

supérbus, -a, -um

taúrus, -ī, m.

tégō, tégere, téxī, téctus

tempéstās, tempestátis, f.

témptō, -áre, -ávī, -átus

ter

térreō, terrére, térruī, térritus

thálamus, -ī, m.

tórqueō, torquére, tórsī, tórtus

tórus, -ī, m.

bull; bullock

(taurine, toreador)

proud, arrogant, insolent

(superb)

storm, tempest; disturbance;
multitude

(tempestuous)

cover, cover over, hide; shelter;
dissemble, keep secret

(tegmen)

three times, thrice

(tertiary)

try, attempt; tempt;
seek, examine

(temptation)

inner room, chamber;
marriage bed

frighten, terrify

(terrible)

sofa, couch, bed

twist, bend, turn

(torque, torture)

tráhō, tráhere, trắxī, tráctus

trémō, trémere, trémuī

trístis, trístis, tríste

Trōs, Trŏis, m.

tū́tus, -a, -um

úterus, -ī, m.

váleō, valére, váluī, valitúrus

várius, -a, -um

vástus, -a, -um

vel

tremble, shake, quake

(tremor)

draw, drag; lead, bring; sweep along;
spend, prolong

(traction)

a Trojan

sad, sorrowful, dejected;
dismal, gloomy

(tristful)

womb; belly

(uterine)

safe, secure

various, variegated;
changing, variable; fickle

(invariable)

be well, be strong;
be able; say goodbye

(valiant)

or, or indeed; certainly

unoccupied; vast, immense, huge

(vastitude)

vélut

vestígium, vestígiī, n.

véstis, véstis, f.

vétus, véteris

vínculum, -ī, n.

vírgō, vírginis, f.

vírtūs, virtútis, f.

víta, -ae, f.

vōs

step, footprint, track;
trace, mark, vestige

(investigate)

just as, even as, like

old, aged; former

(veteran)

clothing, attire, garments;
robe

(vestibule)

young woman, girl

(virgin)

chain, rope, fetter; bond

life

(vital)

strength, courage, excellence;
character, virtue

you *(pl.)*

VERGIL'S METER
The Dactylic Hexameter*

Vergil used dactylic hexameter, the meter of epic poetry, to compose the *Aeneid*. Homer (8th century BC) established the epic character of dactylic hexameter by using it to compose the *Iliad* and the *Odyssey*; many other early Greek epic poems, now lost, were composed in the same meter. Beginning in the third century BC, Roman poets began to experiment with adapting dactylic hexameter to their language. This was no easy task—Greek has a much larger vocabulary, including many more words with multiple short syllables, than does Latin, and is therefore better suited than Latin to dactylic hexameter. Vergil is generally considered by scholars and other admirers to have been the first to bring dactylic hexameter to perfection in Latin; in fact, many believe that he was the first *and* last Latin poet to do so. Whether this is true or not, there is no better introduction to Latin meter than through Vergil; and, strained and odd-sounding though the results may be at first, it is in fact possible with practice to get a reasonable idea of how Latin poetry might have sounded two thousand years ago. It is important to make this attempt both for its own sake and because much ancient poetry, including the *Aeneid*, was intended to be heard; and a well-read excerpt can be quite powerful.

The term **dactylic hexameter** is derived from Greek. **Hexameter** means "six measures" (**hex**, "six"; **metron**, "measure"). A **dactyl** is a measure consisting of one long and two short syllables; the name **dactyl** comes from the Greek word for "finger" (**daktylos**), since with its two joints a finger can be imagined as consisting of one longer and two shorter sections. A line of dactylic hexameter consists of five dactylic measures (or, as they are commonly called, "feet") followed by a final measure of two syllables, the first of which is always long. Any of the five dactyls can be replaced by a **spondee** (a measure consisting of two long syllables). The pattern of long and short syllables in dactylic hexameter looks like this (*Aen.* 1.1–11):

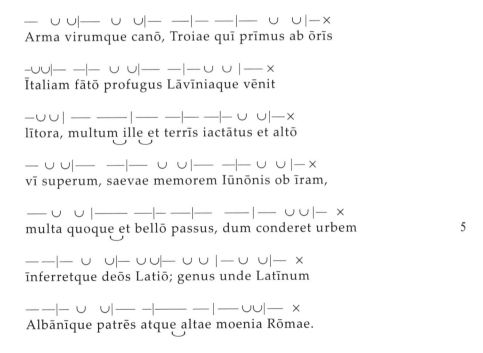

5

* This discussion is taken from *Vergil's Aeneid: Selections from Books 1, 2, 4, 6, 10, and 12*, 2nd edition, by Barbara Weiden Boyd (Wauconda, Ill.: Bolchazy-Carducci Publishers, 2004).

— ∪ ∪|— —|— ∪ ∪|— —|— ∪ ∪|— ×
Mūsa, mihī causās memorā, quō nūmine laesō

— ∪ ∪|— —|— ∪ ∪|— —|— ∪ ∪|— ×
quidve dolēns rēgīna deum tot volvere cāsūs

— —|— ∪∪|— ∪ ∪|— ∪ ∪|— ∪ ∪|— ×
īnsignem pietāte virum, tot adīre labōrēs   10

— ∪ ∪|— —|— ∪ ∪|— —|— ∪ ∪ |— ×
impulerit. Tantaene animīs caelestibus īrae?

Note that the final syllable in a line is always indicated by ×. It can be either long or short; its Latin name, **syllaba anceps**, means "ambiguous" or "undecided syllable."

Most lines of hexameter consist of a combination of dactyls and spondees. The variety of combinations available would have kept the spoken verse from sounding monotonous. Note, however, that lines consisting entirely of spondees are very rare, and that Vergil uses a spondee in the fifth foot only on rare occasions. Such lines (i.e., those with a fifth-foot spondee) are called "spondaic lines," or **spondeiazontes** (singular, **spondeiazon**). Lines consisting entirely of dactyls are relatively unusual as well, although they are not as rare as spondaic lines.

Latin meter is **quantitative**. Every syllable in a Latin word has a quantity, either "long" or "short." Syllable length is determined a) by nature or b) by position. A syllable is long by *nature* if it contains a long vowel or diphthong. A syllable is long by *position* if it contains a vowel followed by a "double" consonant letter (*x* or *z*); or by two distinct consonants, except when the second of these two consonants is *l* or *r*. Neither of these two consonants is usually separated from the consonant that precedes it when pronounced, and therefore does not constitute a lengthening consonant in Latin meter (e.g., in the phrases *aurea clamor* [11.832] and *voce precatur* [11.784], the double consonants *cl-* and *pr-* are pronounced as one sound, and do not lengthen the preceding vowel). The double consonants -*ll*- and -*rr*-, however, do function as true double consonants and so cause the lengthening of the preceding syllable by position (e.g., the words *bellum, currus*).

Some special features of the Latin hexameter should be noted:

Elision – when one word ends with a vowel, diphthong, or –m, and the following word begins with a vowel or h-, the first vowel or diphthong is elided, i.e., blended, with the second. The length of the resulting combination syllable will generally be whatever the length of the second syllable originally was. There are examples of elision above in lines 3, 5, 7, and 11.

Hiatus – see the list of rhetorical and stylistic devices below.

Consonantal vowels – when used in combination with other vowels (e.g., *Iuppiter, coniunx, genua*), the vowels –i- and –u- can sometimes serve as consonants, pronounced as –j- and –w-, respectively. As such, they do not create diphthongs with the vowels next to them, and they can lengthen a preceding short syllable if combined with another consonant. There is an example above in line 2, *Laviniaque*, where the second –i- is treated as a consonant.

Synizesis - see the list of rhetorical and stylistic devices below.

Hypermetric lines – occasionally a hexameter ends with a syllable that can elide with the first syllable of the next line. This final syllable is not needed to complete the metrical pattern of the line in which it appears.

GLOSSARY OF RHETORICAL TERMS,
FIGURES OF SPEECH, AND METRICAL DEVICES*

The following definitions are for the most part based on those found in Pharr's edition of *Aeneid* 1–6. Note, however, that several terms are new to the list, and in one case a term has been redefined.

ALLITERATION is the repetition of the same letter or sound, usually at the beginning of a series of words, as at *Aen.* 1.124, *Interea* **m**agno **m**isceri **m**urmure pontum. **ALLITERATION** is often used in combination with **ONOMATOPOIEA** (see below), as in this example.

ANAPHORA is the repetition of a word or words at the beginning of successive clauses. E.g., *Aen.* 10.429, **Sternitur** *Arcadiae proles,* **sternuntur** *Etrusci.* In Vergil, **ANAPHORA** is often used in combination with **ASYNDETON** (see below), as in this example.

ANASTROPHE is the inversion of the normal order of words, as at *Aen.* 4.320, **te propter.**

APOSIOPESIS ("a falling silent") is a breaking off in the middle of a sentence, the syntax of which is never resumed. E.g., *Aen.* 1.135, **Quos ego—sed motos praestat componere fluctus**, when Neptune decides to suppress his wrath, at least temporarily.

APOSTROPHE is a sudden break from the previous narrative for an address, in the second person, of some person or object, absent or present. E.g., *Aen.* 10.507, **O dolor atque decus magnum rediture parenti,** addressed to the dead Pallas.

ASYNDETON is the omission of conjunctions, as at *Aen.* 12.888, **ingens arboreum.**

CHIASMUS is an arrangement of words in a mirroring, or ABBA, pattern, found most often with pairs of nouns and adjectives. E.g., *Aen.* 1.184, **Navem** *in conspectu* **nullam, tres** *litore* **cervos;** see *Aen.* 1.209 for an example involving nouns and verbs.

ECPHRASIS is an extended and elaborate description of a work of art, a building, or a natural setting. E.g., *Aen.* 6.20–33, describing the scenes on the doors of the temple of Apollo at Cumae.

ELLIPSIS is the omission of one or more words which must be logically supplied in order to create a grammatically complete expression. E.g., *Aen.* 6.122–23, *Quid Thesea, magnum / quid* **memorem** *Alciden?*, where the verb **memorem** must be employed twice, once in each clause.

ENALLAGE is the transference of an epithet from the word to which it strictly belongs to another word connected with it in thought. E.g., *Aen.* 10.444, **socii** *cesserunt* **aequore iusso** = **socii** *cesserunt* **aequore iussi**, where the participle **iusso** takes the place of the more prosaic **iussi**.
(N.B.: this definition is sometimes mistakenly given in textbooks and notes for a related but not identical figure of speech, **HYPALLAGE**. The figure of speech sometimes called **HYPALLAGE** is identical to **METONYMY** [see below].)

ENJAMBMENT is the continuation of a unit of thought beyond the end of one verse and into the first few feet of the next. E.g., *Aen.* 2.12–13, *quamquam animus meminisse horret metuque refugit /* **incipiam**, where *incipiam* completes the meaning of the preceding line; a strong pause follws immediately thereafter.

* This glossary is taken from *Vergil's Aeneid: Selections from Books 1, 2, 4, 6, 10, and 12,* 2nd edition, by Barbara Weiden Boyd (Wauconda, Ill.: Bolchazy-Carducci Publishers, 2004).

EPANALEPSIS is the repetition of a word (often a proper name) in successive clauses or lines of verse for dramatic and/or emotional effect. (It can sometimes appear incombination with ANAPHORA and ASYNDETON [see above for both terms].) E.g., *Aen.* 12.896–97, *Nec plura effatus* **saxum** *circumspicit ingens,* / **saxum** *antiquum ingens, ...*

EUPHEMISM is the avoidance of a direct, sometimes blunt manner of speaking in favor of a more subtle and sometimes diluted form of expression. E.g., *Aen.* 1.219, the circumlocution **extrema pati** instead of the explicit **mori**.

HENDIADYS is the expression of an idea by means of two nouns connected by a conjunction instead of by a noun and a modifying adjective, or by one noun modified by another. E.g., *Aen.* 10.422, **fortunam atque viam = fortunam viae.**

HIATUS is the avoidance in meter of elision between one word ending in a vowel and another beginning with a vowel (or h). E.g., *Aen.* 4.667, **femineo ululatu**. Here as often the metrical device enhances **Onomatopoiea** (see below).

HYPERBATON is the distanced placement of two words which are logically meant to be understood together. E.g., *Aen.* 12.941–42, **infelix** *umero cum apparuit alto* / **balteus**, where the epithet-noun combination **infelix balteus** is dislocated, and added emphasis is thus given to each word.

HYPERBOLE is exaggeration for rhetorical effect. E.g., *Aen.* 1.103, *fluctusque ad sidera tollit.*

HYSTERON PROTERON is the reversal of the natural or logical order of ideas. E.g., *Aen.* 2.258–59, *inclusos utero* **Danaos et** *pinea furtim* / **laxat claustra** *Sinon*, where, contrary to logic, the Greeks are said to be released from the horse *before* it is opened.

LITOTES is understatement, often enhanced by the use of the negative. E.g., *Aen.* 6.170, **non inferiora** *secutus.*

METONYMY is the substitution of one word for another which it suggests. E.g., *Aen.* 10.479, **robur = hasta.**

ONOMATOPOEIA is the use of words of which the sound suggests the sense. E.g., *Aen.* 12.928–29, *totusque* **remugit** *mons circum.*

PATHETIC FALLACY is the attribution of human emotion to inanimate objects. E.g., *Aen.* 6.53, **attonitae** *magna ora domus*, where the dwelling of the Sibyl is described as "awestruck," when in fact awe is felt by those who observe it. When used with adjectives, PATHETIC FALLACY is a special type of TRANSFERRED EPITHET (see below).

PLEONASM is exceptional (and usually unnecessary) fullness of expression, typical of archaic Latin style. E.g., *Aen.* 2.524, **ore effata.**

POLYPTOTON is the repetition of a noun or pronoun in different cases at the beginning of successive phrases or clauses. E.g., *Aen.* 6.166, **Hectoris** *hic magni fuerat comes,* **Hectora** *circum ...* POLYPTOTON is a form of ANAPHORA, and often is found with ASYNDETON (see above).

POLYSYNDETON is an overabundance of conjunctions, as at *Aen.* 1.85–86, *una Eurus***que** *Notus***que** *ruunt creber***que** *procellis* / *Africus ...*

RHETORICAL QUESTION is a question that anticipates no real answer. E.g., *Aen.* 12.793 (Jupiter to Juno): **"Quae iam finis erit, coniunx?"**

Prolepsis is the inclusion in the main story of references to events which in fact will occur after the dramatic time of the poem, and to the people and circumstances involved in these later events. E.g., *Aen.* 6.847–50, **Excudent … ducent … orabunt … describent … dicent**, all used to describe the Romans who will be descended from Aeneas and who are not themselves characters in the *Aeneid*.

Simile is a figure of speech which likens or asserts an explicit comparison between two different things. E.g., *Aen.* 10.454–56, **utque leo, specula cum vidit ab alta . . . haud alia est Turni venientis imago.**

Synchysis is interlocking word order; many variations on the pattern *abAB* exist. E.g., *Aen.* 4.388, **His medium dictis sermonem.**

Synecdoche is the use of a part for the whole, or the reverse. E.g., *Aen.* 10.430, *et vos, O Grais* **imperdita corpora,** *Teucri,* where **corpora** is used of persons.

Synizesis is a metrical effect whereby two contiguous vowels within the same word and normally pronounced separately are slurred into one syllable. E.g., *Aen.* 1.120, **Ilionei**, where the last two vowels, normally pronounced as a short vowel followed by a long, become one long vowel.

Tmesis ("splitting") is the separation into two parts of a word normally written as one, often for a (quasi-)visual effect. E.g., *Aen.* 2.218–19, *bis collo squamea* **circum / terga dati**, where **circum** + **dati** = **circumdati**; the word **terga** is literally "surrounded" by the two parts of **circumdati**.

Transferred Epithet is an epithet which has been transferred from the word to which it strictly belongs to another word connected with it in thought. E.g., *Aen.* 10.426, **tanta caede** = **tanti viri caede**.
(see also **Enallage** [above], an ancient name for the same stylistic feature.)

Tricolon crescens is the accumulation of three parallel phrases or clauses, each of which is at least one syllable longer than that preceding it. E.g., *Aen.* 4.307–9, **Nec te noster amor** [6 syllables] **nec te data dextera quondam** [9 syllables] / **nec moritura tenet crudeli funere Dido?** [15 syllables]. **Tricolon crescens** is often found in combination with **Anaphora** and **Asyndeton** (see above).

Zeugma is the joining of two words by a modifying or governing word which strictly applies to only one of them. E.g., *Aen.* 12.898, *limes agro positus* **litem** *ut* **discerneret arvis**, where zeugma occurs in the use of the verb **discerneret** with both **litem** and **arvis:** the boundary stone *settles* disagreements by *dividing* the fields.

COMPLETE AP* VERGIL VOCABULARY

(I have used *An Elementary Latin Dictionary* by Charlton Lewis to determine the length of vowels.)

A

ā, ab *prep.* from, away from, by (+*abl.*)

Abās, antis *m.* Trojan leader (1.121); Etruscan warrior (10.427)

abdō, ere, didī, ditus put away, hide, shut up

abeō, īre, iī (īvī), itus go away, depart, withdraw, deviate

abiēs, etis *f.* spruce, fir

abluō, ere, luī, lūtus wash off, purify; cleanse

abnuō, ere, nuī, nuitūrus refuse, decline, reject

abripiō, ere, ripuī, reptus snatch away, snatch, seize

abrumpō, ere, rūpī, ruptus break off, destroy, violate

abscessus, ūs, m. departure, absence

abscondō, ere, condī, conditus put away, conceal, hide

absēns, entis absent, distant, left behind

absistō, ere, stitī withdraw, depart from; cease;

abstineō, ēre, tinuī, tentus hold back, refrain

abstrūdō, ere, trūsī, trūsus thrust away; hide

absum, esse, āfuī, āfutūrus be absent or away from; be wanting

ac *conj.* and, and also

Acamās, antis *m.* one of the Greeks at Troy

accēdō, ere, cessī, cessus come or draw near, go to, approach

accendō, ere, cendī, cēnsus set on fire; inflame; arouse; inspire

accersō (*same as* **arcessō**)

accingō, ere, cinxī, cinctus gird, equip, make ready; pitch in

accipiō, ere, cēpī, ceptus receive, accept, admit, welcome

accumbō, ere, cubuī, cubitus recline at, take one's place at the table

accumulō (1) heap up, honor

ācer, ācris, ācre sharp, keen, fierce, violent

acervus, ī *m.* pointed pile, heap

Acestēs, ae *m.* king of Sicily

Achātēs, ae *m.* Aeneas's constant companion

Acherōn, tis *m.* river of the underworld

Achillēs, is *m.* greatest of the Greek heroes at Troy

Achīvus, a, um Greek, Greeks (*pl.*)

aciēs, ēī *f.* sharp edge; battle line; eyesight

acūtus, a, um sharpened, sharp, pointed, jagged

ad *prep.* to, toward, near, at, by (+*acc.*)

addenseō, ēre thicken, pack densely

addō, ere, didī, ditus give in addition, put to, add, lend

adeō *adv.* to that degree, so

adeō, adīre, adiī (īvī), itus go to, approach, reach visit, encounter, meet

adfātus, ūs *m.* speech, address

adflīgō, ere, īxī, īctus shatter, cast down

adflō (1) breath upon, inspire

adfluō, ere, ūxī, uxus flow to, come to

adfor, fārī, fātus address, speak to

adgredior, ī, gressus approach, go to; attack

adhūc *adv.* hitherto, till now, as yet

adiciō, ere, iēcī, iectus throw at, add

adigō, ere, ēgī, āctus drive to, drive, hurl, force

adimō, ere, ēmī, ēmptus take to oneself, take away, snatch away

aditus, ūs *m.* approach, audience, entrance

adiūrō (1) call to witness, swear by

adiuvō, āre, iūvī, iūtus aid, assist, help

adlābor, ī, lapsus glide to

adloquor, ī, locūtus address, speak to

admīror, ārī, ātus wonder at, be surprised at

admoneō, ēre, uī, itus warn, admonish, remind

admoveō, ēre, mōvī, mōtus move or bring to, offer

adnītor, ī, nīxus strive, lean on

adnuō, ere, uī nod, assent, promise

adōrō (1) pray to, worship, adore

adquīrō, ere, quīsīvī, quīsītus acquire, gain

a(d)servō (1) guard, watch

a(d)siduus, a, um constant, unceasing

a(d)sistō, ere, astitī stand by, attend; make a stand

a(d)spectō (1) look at, look towards, overlook

a(d)spectus, ūs *m.* sight, view, appearance

a(d)spiciō, ere, spexī, spectus look at, look upon, behold; regard

adstō, āre, adstitī stand near; be at hand, look on; stand up

adsum, esse, fuī, futūrus be present, be at hand, near

adsurgō, ere, rēxī, rēctus rise up, stand up, rise

adultus, a, um adult, full grown

advena, ae *m./f.* stranger, foreigner

adveniō, īre, vēnī, ventus come to, come, arrrive

adversor, ārī, ātus oppose, resist

adversus, a, um turned toward, opposing, facing, adverse

advertō, ere, tī, sus turn toward, give heed, note, notice

advolō (1) fly to, fly towards

advolvō, ere, volvī, volūtus roll to or toward

adytum, ī *n.* sanctuary, shrine, tomb

Aeacidēs, ae *m.* descendant of Aeacus, i.e. Achilles

aedēs, is *f.* hearth; apartments; house, dwelling (*pl.*)

aedificō (1) build, construct

aeger, aegra, aegrum sick, diseased, weary, weak

aemulus, a, um rivaling, competing

Aeneadae, (ār)um *m. pl.* followers of Aeneas

Aenēās, ae *m.* hero of the Aeneid

Aenēius, a, um of Aeneas

aēnum, ī *n.* kettle, cauldron

aēnus, a, um of bronze, brazen

Aeolia, ae *f.* an island near Sicily, abode of Aeolus

Aeolides, ae *m.* son or descendant of Aeolus

Aeolus, ī *m.* god of the winds

aequaevus, a, um of the same or equal age

aequō (1) make equal, adjust, equal, match, do justice to

aequor, oris *n.* the sea, surface of the sea, a level surface

aequus, a, um even, level, just, fair

āēr, āeris, *m.* air, breeze, mist, cloud

aerātus, a, um made of or covered with bronze; brazen

aereus, a, um made of or plated with bronze; brazen

āerius, a, um airy, high, lofty, towering

aes, aeris *n.* copper, bronze

aestās, ātis *f.* summer, summer air

aestus, ūs *m.* heat, flame; tide, sea, flood

aetās, ātis *f.* age; old age; years, time

aeternus, a, um everlasting, eternal

aethēr, eris *m.* upper air, heaven; sky,

aetherius, a, um of the ether, of heaven

aevum, ī *n.* age, time; old age

Āfrica, ae *f.* Northern Africa

Āfricus, ī *m.* the southwest wind

Agathyrsī, ōrum *m. pl.* people of Scythia

Agēnor, oris *m.* a king of Phoenicia and ancestor of Dido

ager, agrī *m.* field, land

agger, eris *m.* heap, mound; elevation; dike; rampart

aggerō (1) heap up, increase

agitātor, ōris *m.* driver, charioteer

agitō (1) drive with violence; chase, torment, harass

agmen, inis *n.* army (on the march), column, train, formation, rank, line

agnōscō, ere, nōvī, nitus recognize

agō, agere, ēgī, āctus drive, do, pursue, conduct; come! (*imperative*)

Āiāx, ācis *m.* a Greek hero, the son of Oileus

ait says, asserts

āla, ae *f.* wing, pinion

ālātus, a, um winged

Alba, ae *f.* Alba Longa, an ancient city of Latium

Albānus, a, um of Alba, Alban

Alcīdēs, ae *m.* descendant of Alcaeus, Hercules

āles, ālitis *m./f.* bird

Alētēs, ae *m.* a friend of Aeneas

aliēnus, a, um another's, foreign

aliquī, qua, quod some, any

aliquis, qua, quid someone, anyone

aliter *adv.* otherwise

alius, a, ud another, other, else

alligō (1) bind, tie, fasten, imprison

almus, a, um nourishing, fostering, propitious, kindly

alō, ere, uī, (i)tus nourish, feed, encourage, strengthen, rear

Alpīnus, a, um of the Alps, Alpine

altāria, ium *n. pl.* altar

alter, tera, terum one of two, the other

alternō (1) do by turns; waver, hesitate

alternus, a, um one after the other; in turn

altum, ī *n.* sea; heaven

altus, a, um high, lofty; deep, profound;

alumnus, ī *m.* nursling, foster-child, child, son

alvus, ī *f.* belly, body

amārus, a, um bitter, unpleasant, unwelcome

Amazonis, idis *f.* an Amazon

ambāgēs, is *f.* turning, winding; riddle, mystery; details

ambio, īre, īvī, ītus go around, surround, encircle, approach

ambō, ae, ō both; two

ambrosius, a, um ambrosial, divine; immortal; lovely

āmēns, entis senseless; frantic, distracted; amazed

amiciō, īre, uī, ictus throw around; wrap, envelop

amictus, ūs *m.* cloak, mantle, robe; veil

amīcus, a, um friendly

amīcus, ī *m.* friend

āmittō, ere, mīsī, missus lose, send away; let go

amnis, is *m.* river, stream; torrent

amō (1) love, cherish, like

amor, ōris *m.* love, affection, fondness; as person - Cupid

amplector, ī, exus enfold, embrace, wind about

amplus, a, um grand, roomy, spacious; splendid, glorious

Amycus, ī *m.* king of the Bebrycians or friend of Aeneas

an *conj.* or **an...an** whether...or

Anchīsēs, ae *m.* Aeneas's father

Anchīsiadēs, ae *m.* descendant of Anchises, Aeneas

ancora, ae *f.* anchor

Androgeōs, eō *m.* son of Minos, the king of Crete

anguis, is *m.* serpent, snake

angustus, a, um narrow

anhēlus, a, um panting, heaving

anima, ae *f.* breath, breath of life; life, existence; shade, soul spirit

animus, ī *m.* soul, spirit, heart, courage, daring, feeling

Anna, ae *f.* Dido's sister

annālis, is *m.* story

annōsus, a, um aged, old

annus, ī *m.* year

ante *prep.+ adv.* before, in front of (+*acc.*); previously

anteferō, ferre, tulī, lātus put before, carry before

Antēnor, oris *m.* Trojan leader, founder of Patavium

Antheus, eī, *acc.* **ea** *m.* friend of Aeneas

antīquus, a, um ancient, aged, former

antrum, ī *n.* cave, cavern, grotto

aper, aprī *m.* wild boar

aperiō, īre, uī, tus open, uncover, disclose, reveal

apex, icis *m.* tip, point, summit

apis, is *f.* bee

Apollō, inis *m.* god of music and prophecy

appāreō, ēre, uī, itum appear, be disclosed, be seen

appellō, ere, pulī, pulsus drive to, bring to

aptō (1) fit, adjust, equip

aqua, ae *f.* water

Aquilō, ōnis *m.* the north wind, wind

aquōsus, a, um watery, rainy, rain-bearing

āra, ae *f.* altar

Ārae, ārum *f. pl.* the Altars, a rock formation in the sea near Africa

arbor, oris *f.* tree, trunk, shoot

arboreus, a, um treelike, branching

arbōs, oris *f.* (*same as* **arbor**)

Arcades, um *m. pl.* Arcadians

Arcadius, a, um of Arcadia

arcānum, ī *n.* secret

arcānus, a, um secret, hidden

arceō, ēre, uī bind, confine, keep off, debar

arcessō, ere, īvī, ītus cause to come, call, summon

Arctos, ī *f.* the North

arcus, ūs *m.* bow, rainbow, curve, bend

ardēns, entis burning, blazing, fiery, flashy

ardeō, ēre, arsī, arsūrus be on fire, burn, blaze

arduus, a, um steep, high, lofty, towering

argentum, ī *n.* silver; silver plate

Argī, ōrum *m. pl.* Greeks

Argīvus, a, um Greek, Argive

Argolicus, a, um of Argos, Greek

arguō, ere, uī, ūtus prove, reveal, betray

āridus, a, um dry, parched

ariēs, etis *m.* ram, battering ram

arma, ōrum *n. pl.* arms, weapons; tools, equipment

armātus, a, um armed, equipped

armentum, ī *n.* cattle for plowing; herd, drove

armiger, erī *m.* armor-bearer

armō (1) equip, arm

armus, ī *m.* shoulder; flank

arō (1) plow, till; inhabit

arrigō, ere, arrēxī, arrēctus direct to, raise, uplift

ars, artis *f.* skill, dexterity; art; practice

artifex, icis *m.* artist, artisan, contriver

artus, a, um close, tight

artus, ūs *m.* joint, limb, frame, body

arvum, ī *n.* plowed land, cultivated field, field

arx, arcis *f.* citadel, fortress, stronghold; hill, peak

Ascanius, (i)ī *m.* Aeneas's son

ascendō, ere, endī, ēnsus climb, mount, ascend

Asia, ae *f.* Asia Minor

asper, aspera, asperum rough; thorny, jagged; harsh

asportō (1) carry away; carry off

Assaracus, ī *m.* former king of Troy, Anchises' grandfather

ast *conj.* but; yet, at least

astrum, ī *n.* star

asȳlum, ī *n.* place of refuge; sanctuary

at *conj.* but; yet, at least

āter, tra, trum black, dark, sable, dusky; gloomy

Atlās, antis *m.* mountain in N. Africa; god who supports the world

atque *conj.* and, and also; but, than

Atrīdēs, ae *m.* a descendant of Atreus, especially Agamemnon or Menelaus

ātrium, (i)ī *n.* court, hall, atrium, room

attollō, ere lift up, raise; rear

attonitus, a, um thunderstruck; awed, amazed, dazed

auctor, ōris *m.* father, progenitor, producer

audēns, entis daring, bold, courageous

audeō, ēre, ausus dare, venture, risk

audiō, īre, īvī, ītus hear, listen to

auferō, auferre, abstulī, ablātus take away, carry off, withdraw, remove

augur, uris *m./f.* seer, soothsayer, diviner, augur

augurium, (i)ī *n.* the observance of omens, augury

aula, ae *f.* courtyard, inner court

Aulis, idis *f.* town on the east coast of Greece

aura, ae *f.* air, breeze, wind, blast

aureus, a, um golden, of gold

auricomus, a, um golden-haired, with golden foliage

aurīga, ae *m./f.* charioteer, driver

auris, is *f.* ear

Aurōra, ae *f.* goddess of dawn

aurum, ī *n.* gold

Ausonius, a, um Ausonian, Italian

auspex, icis *m./f.* an interpreter of omens given by birds, diviner, augur

auspicium, (i)ī *n.* divination by the flight of birds, auspices; wishes

Auster, trī *m.* the south wind

ausum, ī *n.* bold act

aut *conj.* or; **aut...aut** either...or

autem *adv.* however, on the other hand

Automedōn, ontis *m.* charioteer of Achilles

auxilium, (i)ī *n.* help, aid, assistance

avārus, a, um greedy, covetous

āvehō, ere, āvcxī, āvectus carry away, take away

āvellō, ere, vellī, vulsus tear away, pluck, snatch away

Avernus, ī *m.* a lake near Cumae (entrance to the underworld); *adj.* of lake Avernus

āvertō, ere, vertī, versus turn away, avert, remove

avidus, a, um eager, greedy, desirous

avis, is *f.* bird

āvius, a, um out of the way, remote, trackless

avus, ī *m.* grandfather

axis, is *m.* axle, heaven, open sky

B

bacchor, ārī, ātus revel; celebrate the festival of Bacchus

Bacchus, ī *m.* god of wine, son of Jupiter and Semele

balteus, ī *m.* belt, sword-belt

barba, ae *f.* beard

barbaricus, a, um foreign, strange, barbaric

Barcaeī, ōrum *m. pl.* inhabitants of Barce, a town in Libya

beātus, a, um happy, blessed, fortunate

bellātrīx, īcis *f.* female warrior

bellō (1) wage war, battle

bellum, ī *n.* war

bene *adv.* well, agreeably

benignus, a, um kind, good, friendly, pleasing

bibō, ere, bibī drink

bidēns, ntis *f.* a sheep, (literally, having two teeth)

biformis, e of double form, two-shaped

bīgae, ārum *f. pl.* a team of two horses, a two-horse chariot

biiugus, a, um two yoked together

bīnī, ae, a two by two, two each

bipennis, is *f.* a two-edged axe, double axe, battle-axe

birēmis, is *f.* a ship with two banks of oars, bireme

bis twice, double

bonus, a, um good

Boreās, ae *m.* the north wind, the North

bracchium, (i)ī *n.* arm; the fore-arm

brattea, ae *f.* thin plate of leaf or metal; metal

brevis, e short, brief

brūma, ae *f.* winter

brūmālis, e wintry

bulla, ae *f.* knob, stud, bubble

Byrsa, ae *f.* citadel of Carthage

C

cadō, ere, cecidī, cāsus fall, fall down, descend

cadus, ī *m.* jar, urn

caecus, a, um blind

caedēs, is *f.* killing, slaughter, murder

caedō, ere, cecīdī, caesus cut, cut down, strike, kill

caelestēs, ium *m./f. pl.* the gods

caelestis, e of heaven, from heaven

caelō (1) engrave, carve

caelum, ī *n.* sky, heaven, the heavens

Caesar, aris *m.* Augustus or Julius Caesar

Caīcus, ī *m.* friend of Aeneas

Cāiēta, ae *f.* town on the coast of Latium

calcar, āris *n.* spur

caleō, ēre, caluī glow, be hot, be warm

calidus, a, um warm, hot

callis, is *m.* a path, mountain-path

calor, ōris *m.* heat, warmth, glow

campus, ī *m.* field, plan, level place

candeō, ēre, uī shine, glitter, glisten

canis, is *m./f.* dog

canō, ere, cecinī, cantus sing (of), sound, play

canōrus, a, um melodious, harmonious

cantus, ūs *m.* song, singing

cānus, a, um white, hoary

capessō, ere, īvī, ītus seize eagerly, snatch at, lay hold of

capiō, ere, cēpī, captus seize, grasp, capture

capra, ae *f.* she-goat

captīvus, a, um captured, captive

capulus, ī *m.* hilt

caput, itis *n.* head, the summit, person

Capys, yos *m.* friend of Aeneas

carbasus, ī *f.* canvas, sail

carcer, eris *m.* prison, jail

cardō, inis *m.* hinge

careō, ēre, uī, itus lack, be free from (+*abl.*)

carīna, ae *f.* keel; ship

carmen, inis *n.* song, poem, verse

carpō, ere, carpsī, carptus pluck, pick, tear away

cārus, a, um dear, precious, valued

Cassandra, ae *f.* daughter of Priam and priestess of Apollo

castīgō (1) correct, chastise, blame, chide

castra, ōrum *n. pl.* military camp

cāsus, ūs *m.* fall, falling-down, ruin, failure

caterva, ae *f.* crowd, troop, throng

Caucasus, ī *m.* chain of mountains between the Black and Caspian Seas

causa, ae *f.* cause, reason, motive

cautēs, is *f.* crag, pointed rock

caverna, ae *f.* cave, cavern, grotto

cavō (1) hollow out, excavate

cavus, a, um hollow, excavated

Cēcropidēs, ae *m. pl.* Athenians (descendants of Cecrops, founder of Athens)

cēdō, ere, cessī, cessus go from, remove, withdraw, abandon

celebrō (1) frequent, crowd, throng, practice, celebrate

celer, eris, ere quick, swift, speedy

celerō (1) quicken, hasten, accelerate

cella, ae *f.* store-room, cell, sanctuary

cēlō (1) hide, conceal from, elude, cover

celsus, a, um lofty, elevated, towering

centum one hundred

Cereālis, e sacred to Ceres

Cerēs, eris *f.* daughter of Saturn, goddess of agriculture

cernō, ere, crēvī, crētus separate, distinguish, discern, perceive

certāmen, inis *n.* contest, struggle, strife

certō (1) fight, contend, struggle

certus, a, um determined, resolved, fixed, certain

cerva, ae *f.* doe, deer (female)

cervīx, īcis *f.* neck, nape

cervus, ī *m.* stag, deer (male)

cessō (1) delay, loiter, do nothing, be slack

cēterī, ōrum *m. pl.* the others, the rest

ceu *adv.* as, like, just as

Chalcidicus, a, um of Chalcis, of Cumae

chlamys, ydis *f.* mantle, military cloak

chorus, ī *m.* troop of dancers, chorus

cieō, ēre, cīvī, citus cause to go, move; rouse, stir, call

cingō, ere, cinxī, cinctus equip, gird oneself; surround, encircle

cingulum, ī *n.* belt, girdle

cinis, cineris *m.* ashes

circā *adv.* around, round about, near

circum *adv.+ prep.* around, all around (+*acc.*)

circumdō, dare, dedī, datus surround, place around, encompass

circumspiciō, ere, spexī, spectus look about, observe

circumstō, stāre, stetī, status stand around, surround

circumveniō, īre, vēnī, ventus encircle, be around

circumvolō (1) fly around

Cithaerōn, ōnis *m.* mountain sacred to Bacchus

cithara, ae *f.* lute, cithara

cito *adv.* quickly

citus, a, um quick, swift, rapid

cīvis *m./f.* citizen

clam *adv.* secretly, covertly

clāmō (1) shout, call, cry out

clāmor, ōris *m.* shout

clārus, a, um clear, bright, famous

classis, is *f.* fleet, division

claudō, ere, clausī, clausus shut, close, enclose

claustrum, ī *n.* bar, bolt, barrier

clipeus, ī *m.* round shield

Cloanthus, ī *m.* friend of Aeneas

Clonus, ī *m.* Clonus, a craftsman

Cnōsius (*same as* **Gnōsius**)

Cōcȳtus, ī *m.* river of the underworld

coeō, īre, iī, itus come together, meet, assemble

coepī, isse, tus begin, commence

coetus, ūs *m.* assemblage, crowd, company

Coeus, ī *m.* one of the Titans

cognōmen, inis *n.* surname, second-name, family-name

cognōscō, ere, nōvī, nitus ascertain, understand, learn, know

cōgō, ere, coēgī, coāctus collect, compel, force, urge

colligō, ere, lēgī, lēctus gather, collect; assemble

collis, is *m.* hill

collum, ī *n.* neck

colō, ere, coluī, cultus till, care for, cultivate; honor, love

colōnus, ī *m.* farmer, settler

color, ōris *m.* color, hue, tint

coluber, brī *m.* snake, serpent

columba, ae *f.* dove, pigeon

columna, ae *f.* pillar, column, post

coma, ae *f.* hair; foliage

comes, itis *m./f.* friend, companion, comrade

comitātus, ūs *m.* escort, crowd, retinue

comitor, ārī, ātus accompany, attend, follow

commendō (1) commit, entrust; command

comminus *adv.* hand to hand, in close contest, near

commisceō, ērē, miscuī, mixtus mix, mingle together, unite

commissum, ī *n.* crime, fault

committō, ere, mīsī, missus join, commit, fight, entrust, practice

commoveō, ērē, mōvī, mōtus shake, stir, trouble; displace, carry away

commūnis, e common, general, universal

cōmō, ere, psī, ptus comb, arrange, braid

compāgēs, is *f.* joint, structure

compellō, ere, pulī, pulsus accost, address; reproach, rebuke

complector, ctī, xus clasp, embrace, grasp

compleō, ēre, ēvī, ētus fill, fill up, cram

compōnō, ere, posuī, positus collect, lay; put to rest, quiet

comprendō, ere, dī, ēnsus take hold of, seize, grasp

cōnātus, ūs *m.* effort, attempt

concēdō, ere, cessī, cessus withdraw; grant; permit

concha, ae *f.* shell

concidō, ere, ī fall, collapse

conciliō (1) bring together, unite

conciō, īre, cīvī, citus move violently, shake

conclāmō (1) shout, acclaim; call loudly

conclūdō, ere, sī, sus close, shut up; restrain, limit, restrict

concrēscō, ere, crēvī, crētus grow together, harden; take form, grow

concurrō, ere, rī, sus assemble, gather, battle, fight

concursus, ūs *m.* throng, mob, tumult, concourse

concutiō, ere, cussī, cussus shake, agitate, shock

condēnsus, a, um dense, close, thick, crowded, drawn together

condō, ere, didī, ditus found, establish, build; bury, hide

cōnfīdō, ere, fīsus sum trust, confide, rely on

cōnfīō, fierī, fectus be arranged, be accomplished

cōnfundō, ere, fūdī, fūsus mingle, mix, blend; pour out; confuse

congerō, ere, gessī, gestus bring together, collect; construct, accumulate

congressus, ūs *m.* meeting, assembly, conference

conicio, ere, iēcī, iectus throw, hurl, thrust; conclude, infer

coniugium, (i)ī *n.* marriage, union

coniungo, ere, iūnxī, iūnctus join, unite, gather

coniunx, iugis *m./f.* spouse, husband, wife

conlābor, ī, lāpsus fall in ruins, crumble, sink

cōnor, ārī, ātus try, attempt, begin

conscendō, ere, dī, sus climb, ascend, mount

conscius, a, um witnessing, privy, knowing, conscious

consīdō, ere, sēdī, sessus settle, sit down, sink down

consilium, (i)ī *n.* council, plan, stratagem

consistō, ere, stitī, stitus stand still, halt, stop, make a stand

conspectus, ūs *m.* sight, view, presence

conspiciō, ere, spexī, spectus perceive, observe, look at

consternō, ere, strāvī, strātus strew, pave, cover

constituō, ere, uī, ūtus decide, establish, determine

consulō, ere, uī, tus reflect, deliberate, consider, resolve

consultum, ī *n.* decree, decision; deliberation

consūmō, ere, psī, ptus use up, eat, devour

consurgō, ere, surrēxī, surrēctus rise, stand up, arise

contendō, ere, tendī, tentus strain, hasten, press on; fight

conticescō, ere, ticuī fall silent, become still

contiguus, a, um bordering, neighboring, adjoining

contingō, ere, tigī, tāctus happen; touch, take hold of, seize, touch, concern

continuō immediately, without delay

contorqueō, ēre, torsī, tortus turn, twist, twirl

contrā *adv.+ prep.* against, opposite, facing (+*acc.*)

contrahō, ere, traxī, tractus collect, assemble, accomplish

contrārius, a um opposite, contrary, opposed

contundō, ere, tudī, tūsus beat, crush, pound

cōnūbium, (i)ī *n.* marriage

convallis, is *f.* valley, ravine

convectō (1) carry together, heap together

convellō, ere, vellī, vulsus tear away, pull off, wrest, rend

conveniō, īre, vēnī, ventus gather, assemble

convertō, ere, vertī, versus turn round reverse; change, alter

convexum, ī *n.* hollow, cavity, recess

convīvium, (i)ī *n.* feast, banquet

convolvō, ere, volvī, volūtus roll together, roll around, fasten together

coorior, īrī, ortus stand up, arise, appear

cōpia, ae *f.* plenty, supply, troops (*pl.*)

cor, cordis *n.* heart

cōram *adv.* in the presence of, openly

corneus, a, um of horn

cornū, ūs *n.* horn, antler; trumpet

corōna, ae *f.* garland, crown

corpus, oris *n.* body

corripiō, ere, ripuī, reptus seize, snatch, grasp; attack

corrumpō, ere, rūpī, ruptus destroy, ruin, lay waste; corrupt

corruō, ere, ruī, — fall down, tumble, sink

coruscō (1) vibrate, tremble, shake, brandish

coruscus, a, um flashing, gleaming, glittering

costa, ae *f.* rib

cothurnus, ī *m.* hunting boot, buskin

crāstinus, a, um tomorrow's

crātēr, ēris *m.* mixing bowl

crēber, bra, brum frequent, thick, close

crēdō, ere, didī, ditus believe, trust, confide in (+*dat.*)

crepitō (1) rattle, creak, rustle

crepitus, ūs *m.* rattling, creaking

crescō, ere, crēvī, crētus grow, increase, rise

Crēsius, a, um Cretan

Crētes, ium *m. pl.* Cretans, people of Crete

Creūsa, ae *f.* Aeneas's wife

crīnis, is *m.* hair

crispō (1) swing, brandish

cristātus, a, um crested, tufted, plumed

croceus, a, um yellow, golden, saffron-colored

crūdēlis, e cruel, unfeeling, hard

cruentus, a, um spotted with blood, bloody, stained

cruor, ōris *m.* blood, bloodshed, gore

cubīle, is *n.* couch, bed, marriage-bed

cubitum, ī *n.* elbow

culmen, inis *n.* top summit, roof, gable

culpa, ae *f.* fault, error, blame, guilt, failure

cum *prep.* with (+*abl.*); *conj.* when, since, although

Cūmae, ārum *f. pl.* town on the coast of Campania

Cūmaeus, a, um of Cumae

cumulō (1) heap, accumulate, pile, overload

cumulus, ī *m.* heap, pile, mass, surplus

cunctor, ārī, ātus delay, linger, hesitate

cūnctus, a, um all, entire, all together

cuneus, ī *m.* wedge

cupīdō, inis *f.* desire, wish, longing

cupiō, ere, īvī, ītus long for, desire, wish

cūr why?

cūra, ae *f.* anxiety, distress, care, concern

cūrō (1) care for, take pains with, attend to

currō, ere, cucurrī, cursus run, hasten

currus, ūs *m.* chariot, car, wagon

cursus, ūs *m.* running course, a run, journey

curvus, a, um crooked, curved, bent

cuspis, idis *f.* point, spear, javelin, lance

custōs, ōdis *m.* guard, overseer, protector

Cyclōpius, a, um of the Cyclops

cycnus, ī *m.* swan

Cyllēnius, m. Mercury; mountain in Arcadia, his birthplace; *adj.* Cyllenean

Cȳmothoē, ēs *f.* a sea nymph

Cynthus, ī *m.* mountain in Delos, the birthplace of Diana and Apollo

Cytherēa, ae *f.* Venus, goddess of Cythera (island in the Aegean near Venus's birthplace)

D

Daedalus, ī *m.* famous artisan, father of Icarus

damnō (1) condemn, convict, blame

Danaüs, a, um of Danaus (famous Greek king), the Greeks (*pl.*)

daps, dapis *f.* feast, banquet

Dardania, ae *f.* Troy, city of Dardanus

Dardanidēs, ae *m.* a descendant of Dardanus, a Trojan ; Trojans (*pl.*)

Dardanius, a, um Trojan, of Dardanus

Dardanus, a, um of Dardanus, Trojan

Daunus, ī *m.* Turnus's father

dē *prep.* from, away from, down from; concerning, according to (+*abl.*)

dea, ae *f.* goddess

dēbellō (1) subdue, quell, vanquish

dēbeō, ēre, uī, itus owe, be in debt; ought

dēcēdō, ere, cessī, cessus go away, withdraw, depart

dēcerpō, ere, cerpsī, cerptus pluck off, tear away, break

decet, ēre, decuit, — it is fitting, it is proper

dēcipiō, ere, cēpī, ceptus catch, ensnare, entrap; deceive

dēclīnō, (1) turn, bend aside, tear away; deflect

dēcurrō, ere, (cu)currī, cursus run down, hasten

decus, oris *n.* grace, glory, honor

dēdūcō, ere, dūxī, ductus lead away, escort, turn aside, drive off

dēfendō, ere, dī, sus defend, protect

dēfensor, ōris *m.* protector, defender

dēferō, ferre, tulī, lātus bear, carry; report

dēfessus, a, um tired, weary, exhausted

dēficiō, ere, fēcī, fectus revolt, desert; fail

dēfīgō, ere, fīxī, fīxus fasten, fix, plant

dēfluō, ere, flūxī, flūxus glide down, fall, descend

dēformō (1) disfigure, spoil, mar

dēfungor, ī, fūnctus discharge, perform, finish

dēgener, eris degenerate, unworthy

dehinc *adv.* henceforth, hereafter, next, then

dehīscō, ere, hīvī, — part, divide, split open

dēiciō, ere, iēcī, iectus throw down, cut down, destroy

deinde *adv.* then, next, thence

Dēiopēa, ae *f.* a nymph

Dēiphobē, ēs, *f.* priestess of Apollo

dēligō, ere, lēgī, lēctus choose, select, designate

Dēlius, a, um of Delos; of Apollo

Dēlos, ī *f.* island in the Aegean, birthplace of Apollo

dēlūbrum, ī *n.* temple, shrine, sanctuary

dēmēns, entis insane, demented, mad, raving, foolish

dēmittō, ere, mīsī, missus let down, drop, let fall, shed

dēmō, ere, mpsī, mptus take away, take off, subtract

dēmum *adv.* at length, at last, finally

dēnī, ae, a ten each, ten at a time

dēnique *adv.* and thereafter, at last, at length, finally

dēns, dentis *m.* tooth; fluke

dēnsus, a, um thick, close, dense, compact

dēpascor, ī, pastus to eat up, feed on

dēprecor, ārī, ātus avert by prayer, deprecate, seek to avoid

dēripiō, ere, ripuī, reptus tear off, tear away, pull down

dēsaeviō, īre, īvī, ītus rage, rave furiously

dēscendō, ere, dī, sus go down, climb down, descend

dēscēnsus, ūs *m.* way down, descent

dēscrībō, ere, scrīpsī, scrīptus transcribe, write down; describe

dēserō, ere, uī, tus leave, forsake, abandon, desert

dēserta, ōrum *n. pl.* waste lands, wilderness

dēsertus, a, um deserted, solitary, lonely

dēsiliō, īre, iluī, ultus jump down, leap down, dismount

dēsinō, ere, sīvī, situs stop, desist, cease

dēsistō, ere, stitī, stitus cease, desist from

dēspectō (1) despise, look down on

dēspiciō, ere, spēxī, spectus despise, look down on, disparage

dēstruō, ere, ūxī, ūctus tear down, raze, demolish

dēsuētus, a, um unaccustomed, unfamiliar, obsolete

dēsum, esse, fuī be away, be absent, fail, be missing

dēsuper *adv.* from above, from overhead

dētineō, ēre, uī, tentus hold back, hold off, keep back, detain, check

dētorqueō, ēre, torsī, tortus bend aside, turn off, twist

dētrūdō, ere, sī, sus thrust away, push down, dislodge, dispossess

deus, ī *m.* god, deity

dēveniō, īre, vēnī, ventus come, arrive, reach

dēvolō (1) fly down

dexter, tra, trum right, to the right; skillful

Diāna, ae *f.* sister of Apollo; goddess of the moon and hunt

diciō, ōnis *f.* dominion, sovereignty, sway, authority, control

dīcō, ere, dīxī, dictus say, speak, sing, describe, name

dicō(1) dedicate, consecrate, devote

Dictaeus, a, um of Dicte, a mountain in Crete

dictum, ī *n.* assertion, remark, saying

Dīdō, ōnis *f.* queen of Carthage

diēs, ēī *m.* day

difficilis, e difficult, hard, troublesome

diffugiō, ere, fūgī, — fly apart, disperse, scatter

diffundō, ere, fūdī, fūsus pour out, pour forth; spread

dignor, ārī, ātus deem worthy, honor, deign

dignus, a, um worthy, deserving, suitable, fitting, proper

dīgredior, ī, gressus go apart, separate, part, go away, depart

dīlābor, ī, lapsus go to pieces, melt away, dissolve, scatter, disperse

dīligō, ere, lēxī, lēctus value, esteem, prize, love; approve

dīmoveō, ēre, mōvī, mōtus part, separate, divide, dislodge

dīrigō, ere, rēxī, rēctus direct

dīripiō, ere, uī, reptus tear apart, ravage, spoil, plunder, pillage

dīrus, a, um ominous, fearful, awful, dreadful, horrible

Dīs, Dītis *m.* Pluto, god of the underworld

discernō, ere, crēvī, crētus separate, divide; distinguish, discern

discessus, ūs *m.* departure, farewell, removal

discolor, ōris of another color, not of the same color; of different colors

discrepō, āre, uī, — differ in sound, be different, vary

discrīmen, inis *n.* distance, distinction, difference; decisive moment, crisis

dīsiciō, ere, iēcī, iectus drive apart, scatter, route; ruin, destroy

disiungō, ere, iūnxī, iūnctus sever, divide, separate, estrange

dispellō, ere, pulī, pulsus scatter, disperse

dissimulō (1) disguise; dissemble, hide, conceal, pretend

dissultō (1) fly in pieces, break apart

distendō, ere, dī, tus swell, stretch out, extend

diū adv. for a long time, all day, continually

dīva, ae *f.* goddess

dīvellō, ere, vellī, vulsus tear apart, separate violently, tear, wrest

dīversus, a, um contrary, opposite, diverse, different

dīves, itis rich, wealthy, opulent

dīvidō, ere, vīsī, vīsus divide, force asunder, part, distribute

dīvīnus, a, um divine

dīvus, a, um of a deity, godlike, divine; god, goddess (*noun*)

dō, dare, dedī, datus give, appoint; grant, bestow; emit, utter

doceō, ēre, uī, ctus teach, instruct, inform

doleō, ēre, uī, itus grieve, suffer, be in pain, lament

Dolopes, um *m. pl.* Dolopians, a people of Thessaly

dolor, ōris *m.* pain, suffering, anguish, distress, grief, trouble

dolus, ī *m.* trickery, artifice; guile, deceit, deception

dominor, ārī, ātus have dominion, domineer, rule

dominus, ī *m.* lord, master, ruler, owner

domō, āre, uī, itus domesticate, tame, break, subdue, conquer

domus, ūs *f.* house, home, dwelling, building

dōnec *conj.* while, as long as; until, at length

dōnum, ī *n.* gift, present

Dōricus, a, um Doric; Greek

dorsum, ī *n.* back; cliff

dōtālis, e of a dowry, dotal

dracō, ōnis *m.* serpent, large serpent, dragon

Dryopes, um *m. pl.* a people in Epirus

dubius, a, um doubtful, uncertain, wavering

dūcō, ere, dūxī, ductus lead, lead away, guide, conduct, prolong; choose

ductor, ōris *m.* leader, commander, general

dulcis, e sweet, agreeable, delightful, agreeable

dum *conj. and adv.* while; until (*with subjunctive*)

duo, ae, o two

duplex, icis twofold, double

duplicātus, a, um doubled, folded

dūrō, (1) harden, solidify; wait, persevere, hold out

dūrus, a, um hard, harsh, vigorous; pitiless, unyielding

dux, ducis *m./f.* leader, guide, general

E

ē, ex *prep.* out of, from; of; since; according to (*+abl.*)

eburnus, a, um of ivory

ecce *demonst. adv.* behold! look!

edāx, ācis greedy, voracious, devouring

edō, edere (ēsse), ēdī, ēsus eat, consume

ēdūcō, ere, dūxī, ductus draw out, take away; bring up, rear

efferō, ferre, extulī, ēlātus carry out, take away; bear, produce

efferus, a, um very wild, fierce, savage

efficiō, ere, fēcī, fectus bring about, effect, cause, produce

effingō, ere, finxī, fīctus wipe clean; form, fashion, mould

effodiō, ere, fōdī, fossus dig out, mine, excavate

effor, ārī, ātus utter, tell, speak out

effugiō, ere, fūgī, — get away, escape; flee from

effundō, ere, fūdī, fūsus pour out, pour forth; abandon

egēns, entis destitute, needy

egēnus, a, um needy, necessitous, destitute

egeō, ēre, uī, — be needy, want, lack, have need (*+abl.*)

ēgerō, ere, gessī, gestus carry out, accomplish

ego I

ēgredior, ī, gressus go out, come forth, go away; disembark, land

ēgregius, a, um distinguished, excellent, eminent

ei *interj.* oh! alas!

ēiciō, ere, iēcī, iectus eject, expel; banish, drive away

ēlābor, ī, lapsus slip away, glide off, escape

elephantus, ī *m.* ivory; an elephant

Elissa, ae *f.* another name for Dido

ēmico, āre, uī, ātus spring out, break forth, leap up

ēminus, a, um aloof, at a distance

ēmittō, ere, mīsī, missus send out; hurl, cast, discharge

emō, emere, ēmī, ēmptus buy, purchase, procure

ēmoveō, ēre, mōvī, mōtus move out, move away, expel

ēn *interj.* lo! behold! see!

Enceladus, ī *m.* a giant

enim *adv.* for, namely, that is to say

ēniteō, ēre, uī, — shine forth, gleam

ēnō (1) swim out; fly

ēnsis, is *m.* sword

ēnumerō (1) count out; recite, recount, describe

eō, īre, īvī, itus go, walk, ride, sail, move

Ēōus, a, um of the dawn, eastern, oriental

Epēos, ī *m.* a Greek warrior at Troy, maker of the horse

epulae, ārum *f. pl.* banquet, feast; sumptuous foods

epulor, ārī, ātus dine, feast, banquet

eques, itis *m.* horseman, rider

equidem *adv.* indeed, truly

equus, ī *m.* horse

Erebus, ī *m.* god of darkness; the underworld

ergō *adv.* therefore, consequently, accordingly

ēripiō, ere, ripuī, reptus tear out, wrest, pluck tear; rescue deliver, free

errō (1) wander, stray, roam; be in error

error, ōris *m.* wandering, winding, meandering, maze

ērubescō, ere, buī, — grow red, blush, feel ashamed

ēruō, ere, uī, utus throw out, take; destroy completely

et *adv. and conj.* and, also

etiam *adv.* also, too, even; still

Etruscī, ōrum *m. pl.* the Etruscans

Euboīcus, a, um of Euboea (an island in the western Aegean)

Eurōpa, ae *f.* Europe

Eurōtās, ae *m.* a river in Laconia

Eurus, ī *m.* southeast or east wind

Eurytidēs, is *m.* son of Eurytus

ēvādō, ere, sī, sus get away, escape; disembark; traverse

Evander, drī *m.* leader of the Arcadians; Pallas's father

ēvānēscō, ere, nuī, — vanish, pass away, disappear

ēvehō, ere, vexī, vectus carry out, proceed, advance

ēveniō, īre, vēnī, ventus come out; happen, result

ēventus, ūs *m.* outcome, result, end, consequence

ēvertō, ere, tī, sus overturn, turn upside down; overthrow, destroy

ēvincō, ere, vīcī, victus overcome, conquer, subdue

ēvocō (1) call out

exanimus, a, um lifeless, dead

exaudiō, īre, īvī, ītus hear clearly, distinguish

excēdō, ere, cessī, cessus leave, depart, go out

excidium, (i)ī *n.* overthrow, demolition, ruin, destruction

excīdō, ere, cīdī, cīsus cut out, hew out

excidō, ere, cidī, — fall out, slip out

exciō, īre, īvī, ītus call out, summon, rouse, awaken

excipiō, ere, cēpī, ceptus take out, withdraw; catch, receive; go on

exclāmō (1) call out, cry aloud, exclaim

excubiae, ārum *f. pl.* watching, keeping watch, watchmen

excūdō, ere, dī, sus strike out, hammer out; prepare, make

excutiō, ere, cussī, cussus shake out, shake off; discard, remove

exeō, īre, iī, itus go out, depart, withdraw; escape

exerceō, ēre, uī, itus employ, busy; occupy

exhālō (1) breath out, exhale

exhauriō, īre, hausī, haustus exhaust, empty; take away

exigō, ere, ēgī, āctus drive out, expel; determine, ascertain; spend

exiguus, a, um small, little, scanty

eximō, ere, ēmī, ēmptus take away, remove; free, release, deliver

exin *adv.* then, after that, next

exitiālis, e destructive, fatal, deadly

exitium, (i)ī *n.* destruction, ruin

exitus, ūs *m.* departure; death; conclusion

exordium, (i)ī *n.* beginning; introduction

exorior, īrī, ortus come out, rise, appear; begin

exōsus, a, um hating, detesting

expediō, īre, īvī, ītus extricate; explain, make clear; arrange

expendō, ere, dī, pēnsus weigh out, weigh; reckon, account; estimate, consider

experior, īrī, pertus try, prove, test, endure; know by experience

expleō, ēre, ēvī, ētus fill up, fill, stuff; pass over, go through; satisfy, appease

explōrō (1) search out, investigate, explore

exposcō, ere, poposcī, — beg, request, entreat, implore

exprōmō, ere, prōmpsī, prōmptus express, state; exhibit, show, display

exquīrō, ere, sīvī, sītus seek out; implore

exsanguis, e bloodless, lifeless; pale, wan

exscindō, ere, scidī, scissus extirpate, annihilate, destroy

exsequor, ī, cūtus follow; fulfill; relate, describe

exsertus, a, um bare, uncovered; projecting

exsilium, (i)ī *n.* exile, banishment

exsolvō, ere, solvī, solūtus deliver, free, set free, liberate

exspectō (1) look out for, await, expect

exspīrō (1) breathe out

exstinguō, ere, nxī, nctus put out, quench, extinguish; abolish, annihilate

exstruō, ere, ūxī, ūctus pile, heap up; build up

exsultō (1) leap up, jump up; boast, indulge

exsuperō (1) mount up, tower; pass over; excel

exta, ōrum *n. pl.* guts, internal organs

extemplō *adv.* immediately, without delay

extendō, ere, dī, tus spread, extend; lengthen; continue

externus, a, um external; foreign, strange

exterritus, a, um terrified, dismayed; made wild

exterus, a, um outside, outer

extrēma, ōrum *n. pl.* death

extrēmus, a, um outermost, utmost, farthest; remotest; last; tip

exuō, ere, uī, ūtus take off, pull off; put away, lay aside

exūrō, ere, ussī, ustus burn up, burn out

exuviae, ārum *f. pl.* spoils; relics; skin

F

fabricātor, ōris *m.* builder, contriver

fabricō (1) build, make, construct, erect

facessō, ere, ī, ītus perform, execute, accomplish

faciēs, ēī, *f.* appearance, form, shape

facilis, e easy

faciō, ere, fēcī, factus make, do, produce, build

factum, ī *n.* deed, act, achievement

fallō, ere, fefellī, falsus trip, fall; err, make a mistake, deceive oneself

falsus, a, um deceptive, false, spurious, delusive

fāma, ae *f.* report, rumor, saying, talk, tradition

Fāma, ae *f.* personification of above

famēs, is *f.* hunger

famula, ae *f.* female slave, maid-servant

far, farris *n.* type of grain; sacrificial meal

fās *n. indecl.* divine law; with **est**, it is lawful

fastīgium, (i)ī *n.* top, summit; roof, battlement

fātālis, e fatal, decreed, ordained, destined

fateor, ērī, fassus confess, grant, acknowledge

fatīgō (1) tire, weary, fatigue, vex, harass

fatīscō, ere fall apart, tumble to pieces

fātum, ī *n.* prediction; fate

faux, faucis *f.* throat, jaws; entrance

fax, facis *f.* torch, flame

fēlīx, īcis happy, fortunate; auspicious

fēmina, ae *f.* woman, female

fēmineus, a, um womanly, feminine

femur, oris *n.* thigh

fenestra, ae *f.* window, opening

fera, ae *f.* wild beast, wild animal

ferīna, ae *f.* venison, game; wild animal flesh

feriō, īre strike, beat; kill

ferō, ferre, tulī, lātus bring, carry, bear, wear; report; offer

ferōx, ōcis wild, bold, warlike

ferrum, ī *n.* iron; iron tool; sword

ferus, a, um wild, untamed, uncultivated

ferveō, ēre glow, steam; burn, rage, rave

fervidus, a, um glowing, fiery, hot, vehement

fessus, a, um tired, fatigued, weary

fēstīnō (1) hurry, hasten; perform

fēstus, a, um festive, joyful, merry

fētus, a, um filled with, pregnant

fētus, ūs *m.* young, offspring; fruit, growth

fībula, ae *f.* clasp, buckle, fastening, brooch

fictus, a, um feigned, fictitious, false

fidēs, ēī *f.* faith, loyalty, belief, reliance; trustworthiness

fidēs, ium *f. pl.* strings, lyre; chords

fīdūcia, ae *f.* trust, confidence

fīdus, a, um loyal, faithful, credible

fīgō, ere, fīxī, fīxus fix, fasten; pierce; plant (steps)

fīlius, (i)ī *m.* son

fīlum, ī *n.* thread, string

fingō, ere, finxī, fictus arrange, touch; suppose, think, conceive

fīnis, is *m.* end, boundary, limit; territory (*pl.*)

fīō, fierī, factus become, be made, happen

firmus, a, um strong, steadfast, enduring

fissilis, e cleft, easily split, fissile

flāmen, inis *n.* wind, gale; priest

flamma, ae *f.* flame, blaze; flame of passion;

flammō (1) kindle, inflame, blaze, burn

flātus, ūs *m.* blowing, breath, snorting

flāvus, a, um golden, yellow, reddish yellow, flaxen-colored

flectō, ere, flēxī, flexus turn, bend, bow; avert; avoid; influence, sway

fleō, ēre, flēvī, flētus weep, cry, lament, wail

flētus, ūs *m.* weeping, wailing, lamenting

flōreō, ēre, floruī, — bloom, blossom, flower; flourish

flōreus, a, um flowery

flōs, flōris *m.* flower, blossom

fluctus, ūs *m.* wave, tide, billow, surge

fluentum, ī *n.* stream, flood

flūmen, inis *n.* stream, river

fluō, ere, flūxī, fluxus flow, pour, throng

fodiō, ere, fōdī, fossus dig, dig up; stab

foedō (1) make foul, defile, pollute

foedus, eris *n.* alliance, compact; marriage contract

foedus, a, um foul, filthy, repulsive; disgraceful

folium, (i)ī *n.* leaf

fōmes, itis *m.* kindling-wood, tinder

fōns, fontis *m.* fountain, spring, source

for, ārī, ātus speak, say; prophesy

foris, is *f.* door, entrance

forma, ae *f.* form, shape; beauty

formīca, ae *f.* ant

fors, fortis *f.* chance, luck, fortune

fors(it)an *adv.* perhaps, it may be that

fortis, e brave, strong, courageous

fortūna, ae *f.* fortune, chance, luck

fortūnātus, a, um lucky, happy, fortunate

foveō, ēre, fōvī, fōtus cherish, fondle, caress

fragor, ōris, *m.* crashing, crash, noise; thunderclap

frāgrāns, ntis fragrant, sweet-smelling

frangō, ere, ēgī, āctus break, shatter, fracture; crush, dishearten

frāter, tris *m.* brother

frāternus, a, um brotherly, fraternal

fraudō (1) cheat, defraud, rob

fraus, fraudis *f.* cheating, deceit, fraud

fraxineus, a, um ashen, of ash wood

fremō, ere, uī, itus roar, resound, howl; applaud; grumble because of

frēnō (1) curb, bridle, restrain, check

frēnum, ī *n.* bridle, curb, bit; restraint

frequēns, ntis regular, constant, repeated; with a throng

frētus, a, um leaning, supporting, relying (on)

frīgidus, a, um cold, cool, chilling

frīgus, oris *n.* coldness, cold, chilliness; cold shudder

frondēns, ntis in leaf, becoming green, leafy

frondēscō, ere put forth leaves; shoot

frondeus, a, um covered with leaves, leafy

frōns, frontis *f.* front, facade; forehead; expression

frōns, frondis *f.* leafy branch, foliage, bough

frūmentum, ī *n.* grain, harvested grain

frūstrā *adv.* in vain, for nothing

frustum, ī *n.* piece, bit

frūx, frūgis *f.* fruit, produce

fūcus, ī *m.* drone, bee

fuga, ae *f.* flight, rapid motion

fugiō, ere, fūgī, fugitūrus flee, run away, escape

fugō (1) cause to flee, put to flight

fulciō, īre, fulsī, fultus prop up, support

fulgeō, ēre, fulsī, — flash, glitter, gleam, shine

fulmen, inis *n.* lightning flash; thunderbolt

fulvus, a, um deep yellow, reddish yellow, tawny

fundāmentum, ī *n.* foundation

fundō, ere, fūdī, fūsus pour, pour out, shed; spread

fundō (1) found, begin; fix, confirm

fungor, ī, fūnctus be engaged, perform, discharge

fūnis, is *m.* rope, cord

fūnus, eris *n.* funeral procession, funeral rites, burial; death, murder

furiae, ārum *f. pl.* the three goddesses of vengeance, the furies

furibundus, a, um raging, mad, furious

furō, ere rage, rave, be out of one's mind

furor, ōris *m.* raving, rage, madness, fury, passion

Furor, ōris *m.* Rage, Madness (*personified*)

fūrtim *adv.* stealthily, secretly, furtively

fūrtīvus, a, um stolen, secret, hidden, concealed, furtive

fūrtum, ī *n.* theft, robbery; secret action, crafty deceit

futūrum, ī *n.* the future

G

Gaetūlus, a, um of the Gaetuli, a North African tribe

galea, ae *f.* helmet

Gallus, a, um of Gaul, Gallic

Ganymēdes, is *m.* Ganymede, Trojan prince, made Jupiter's cupbearer

Garamantis, idis of the Garamantes, a North African tribe

gaudeō, ēre, gāvīsus rejoice, be glad

gaudium, (i)ī *n.* joy, delight

gaza, ae *f.* treasure

gelidus, a, um icy cold, icy, frosty

geminus, a, um twin

gemitus, ūs *m.* groan, sighing, complaint

gemō, ere, uī, itus groan, sigh, lament; bewail

gena, ae *f.* cheek

genetrīx, īcis *f.* mother

genitor, ōris *m.* father

gēns, gentis *f.* race, clan; descendant, offspring

genū, ūs *n.* knee

genus, eris *n.* race, stock, family; birth, noble birth; descendant

germāna, ae *f.* sister

germānus, ī *m.* brother

gerō, ere, gessī, gestus bear, carry, wage; wear

gestō (1) bear, carry, wear, wield

gignō, ere, genuī, genitus give birth to, produce, bear, bring forth

glaciēs, ēī *f.* ice

Glaucus, ī *m.* Glaucus, a Lycian ally of the Trojans

glomerō (1) collect; gather

glōria, ae *f.* glory, fame, honor, praise

Gnōsius, a, um of Gnosus, a city in Crete

gradior, ī, gressus step, walk to, advance

gradus, ūs *m.* step, pace, gait, walk; steps (*pl.*)

Grāius, a, um Greek

grāmen, inis *n.* grass; plant, herb

grandaevus, a, um aged, old

grandis, e full-grown, grown up, old; ripe

grandō, inis *f.* hail, hailstorm

grātēs, ium *f. pl.* thanks, thanksgiving

grātus, a, um dear, acceptable, pleasing, agreeable

gravidus, a, um filled, full, swollen

gravis, e heavy, weighty, burdened

gremium, (i)ī *n.* lap, bosom

gressus, ūs *m.* step, course, way

grex, gregis *m.* flock, herd, drove, swarm

Grȳnēus, a, um of Grynia, site of a temple of Apollo

gurges, itis *m.* whirlpool, gulf

gustō (1) taste, enjoy

Gyās, ae *m.* friend of Aeneas

H

habēna, ae *f.* rein

habeō, ēre, uī, itus have, hold, support, carry; consider, regard

habilis, e manageable, suitable, fit, proper

habitus, ūs *m.* appearance, presence; dress, attire

hāc *adv.* here, there

hāctenus *adv.* thus far, to this place, so far; till now

haereō, ēre, haesī, haesus cling, stick, be fastened; linger, pause

Halaesus, ī *m.* Halaesus, (Italian warrior and enemy of the Trojans)

hālitus, ūs *m.* breath, exhalation

hālō (1) breathe, emit vapor, be fragrant

Hammōn, ōnis *m.* Libyan god identified with Jupiter

harēna, ae *f.* sand; shore, beach

harēnōsus, a, um sandy, full of sand

Harpalycē, ēs *f.* Thracian princess, famous huntress and warrior

harundō, inis *f.* reed; arrow

hasta, ae *f.* spear, lance, javelin

hastīle, is *n.* spear-shaft, javelin-shaft

haud *adv.* not, not at all, by no means

hauriō, īre, hausī, haustus drain, shed; pluck out, swallow, devour, consume

Hebrus, ī *m.* a river in Thrace

Hecatē, ēs *f.* goddess of the underworld

Hector, oris *m.* Troy's champion, son of Priam

Hectoreus, a, um of Hector

Hecuba, ae *f.* Priam's wife

herba, ae *f.* grass, turf

hērēs, ēdis *m./f.* heir, successor

hērōs, ōis *m.* hero, demigod

Hesperia, ae *f.* Western Land, Italy

Hesperius, a, um western, Hesperian; Italian

heu *interj.* alas!

heus *interj.* hey! ho!

hīberna, ōrum *n. pl.* winter quarters, years

hībernus, a, um wintry, of winter

hīc *adv.* here

hic, haec, hoc this, the latter

hiems, hiemis *f.* winter; storm

hinc *adv.* from this place, hence; on either side

homō, inis *m./f.* person, human being, man

honor, ōris *m.* honor, repute, esteem, distinction

honos (*same as* **honor**)

hōra, ae *f.* hour

horrendus, a, um dreadful, terrible, fearful

horrēns, ntis bristly, shaggy, rough

horreō, ēre, uī, — stand on end, bristle; tremble, dread

horrēscō, ere, horruī, — rise on end, stand erect; shudder, tremble

horridus, a, um terrible, wild, savage

horror, ōris *m.* shaking, trembling, shudder; dread, terror, horror

hortor, ārī, ātus urge, press, incite, encourage, exhort

hospes, itis *m./f.* host, guest, visitor, friend

hospitium, (i)ī *n.* hospitality, friendship

hospitus, a, um hospitable; strange, foreign

hostia, ae *f.* victim, sacrifice, sacrificial animal

hostīlis, e enemy's, hostile

hostis, is *m./f.* enemy, foe, stranger

hūc *adv.* to this place, here; to this point, so far

humilis, e lowly, humble, needy, poor

humō (1) bury, inter

humus, ī *f.* earth, ground, soil

hymenaeus, ī *m.* wedding, marriage ceremony

Hyrcānus, a, um Hyrcanian, a people near the Caspian Sea

I

iaceō, ēre, iacuī, iacitus lie, be prostrate, lie at rest

iaciō, ere, iēcī, iactus throw, hurl, scatter

iactō (1) throw out; consider, discuss; pronounce, speak; boast

iaculor, ārī, ātus throw, hurl

iam *adv.* now, at this time, already; with a neg., longer, more

iamdūdum *adv.* long since, long before, for some time now

iānua, ae *f.* door, entrance

Iarbās, ae *m.* king of the Gaetuli in N. Africa

iaspis, idis *f.* jasper (green precious stone)

ibi *adv.* there, in that place; thereupon

ibīdem *adv.* in the same place

Īcarus, ī *m.* Daedalus' son (flew too high)

īcō, ere, īcī, ictus strike, hit, stab, sting

ictus, ūs *m.* blow, stab, cut, wound; force

Īda, ae *f.* mountain near Troy

īdem, eadem, idem the same

ideō *adv.* therefore, for that reason

ignārus, a, um ignorant, inexperienced, unaware

ignāvus, a, um lazy, slothful, idle, sluggish

igneus, a, um fiery, on fire, burning-hot

ignis, is *m.* fire

ignōbilis, e unknown, undistinguished; of low birth, ignoble

ignōtus, a, um unknown, strange, unrecognized; unfamiliar

īlex, icis *f.* oak, holm-oak

Īlia, ae *f.* another name for Rhea Silvia, mother of Romulus and Remus

Īliacus, a, um of Ilium, Trojan

Īlias, adis *f.* a Trojan woman

īlicet *adv.* at once, immediately

Īlioneus, eī *m.* spokesman for the Trojans

Īlium, (i)ī *n.* Troy

Īlius, a, um of Ilium, Trojan

ille, illa, illud that; he, she, it; the former

illīc *adv.* there, in that place

illinc *adv.* from that place, thence

illūc *adv.* to that place, thither

Illyricus, a, um of Illyria, region east of the Adriatic

Īlus, ī *m.* Ascanius' previous name

imāgō, inis *f.* image; ghost, vision; reminder

Imāon, Imāonos *m.* an Italian friend of Halaesus

imbellis, e unwarlike, unfit for war

imber, bris *m.* rain; the sea, water

immānis, e huge; monstrous, frightful

immemor, oris unmindful, heedless

immēnsus, a, um immeasurable, boundless, huge

immergō, ere, sī, sus dip, immerse, submerge

immineō, ēre overhang, command

immītis, e rough, harsh, severe

immittō, ere, mīsī, missus send in, admit; let go, loose

immolō (1) sprinkle with sacrificial meal, sacrifice

immōtus, a, um motionless; unmoved, steadfast, firm

impār, aris uneven, unequal; overmatched

impellō, ere, pulī, pulsus strike against, strike, push; set in motion; force

impēnsus, a, um vast, vehement

imperditus, a, um not destroyed, not slain

imperium, (i)ī *n.* command, order; supreme power, sovereignty

impius, a, um irreverent, wicked, impious

implācābilis, e implacable, irreconcilable

impleō, ēre, ēvī, ētus fill, sate, satisfy

implicō, āre, uī (āvī), itus (ātus) entangle, entwine, embrace, grasp

impōnō, ere, posuī, positus place upon, put on

imprimo, ere, pressī, pressus press upon, press against; emboss, engrave

improbus, a, um wicked, shameless, bad

imprōvidus, a, um off guard; reckless, careless

impūne *adv.* without punishment, with impunity

īmus, a, um lowest, deepest, last; the bottom of

in *prep.* into, to; against (+*acc.*); in, on, upon (+*abl.*)

inānis, e useless, empty, meaningless

incautus, a, um incautious, inconsiderate, heedless

incēdō, ere, cessī, cessus advance, march, proceed

incendō, ere, dī, sus set fire to, burn; rouse, incite

inceptum, ī *n.* undertaking, endeavor

incertus, a, um unsettled, doubtful, uncertain

incessus, ūs, *m.* walking, pace, gait; step

incestō (1) pollute, defile

incīdō, ere, cīdī, cīsus cut into, cut through

incido, ere, cidī, cāsus fall, sink, strike

incipio, ere, cēpī, ceptus begin

inclūdō, ere, sī, sus shut up, confine, enclose

inclutus, a, um famous, renowned

incōgnitus, a, um unknown, untraced

incubō, āre, uī (āvī), itus (ātus) lie upon, rest on; brood over, watch over

incultus, a, um uncultivated, abandoned

incumbō, ere, cubuī, cubitus lean, press; bend to; oppress

incūsō (1) accuse, blame

incutiō, ere, cussī, cussus strike into, inflict; produce

indāgō, inis *f.* net, snare

inde *adv.* from there, thence; thereafter

indēbitus, a, um not owed, not due

indigena, ae native

Indiges, getis *m.* deified hero, patron deity

indignor, ārī, ātus deem unworthy, despise, resent

indignus, a, um unworthy, undeserving; shameful

indulgeō, ēre, lsī, ltus concede, grant, allow

induō, ere, uī, ūtus put on assume; clothe, dress; pierce

inermis, e unarmed, defenseless

iners, ertis helpless, weak

inexpertus, a, um without experience, untested

inextrīcābilis, e inextricable, not to be unraveled

īnfabricātus, a, um unshaped, rough, unwrought

īnfandus, a, um unspeakable, abominable

īnfectus, a, um not done, unaccomplished

īnfēlīx, īcis unfortunate, unlucky, miserable; barren

īnfēnsus, a, um hostile, inimical

īnferior, ius lower, further down; inferior

īnfernus, a, um lower, under; underground

īnferō, ferre, tulī, illātus bring to, carry in, wage; advance (*refl.*)

īnfestus, a, um made unsafe, disturbed; hostile, dangerous

īnfīgō, ere, fīxī, fīxus fasten, implant, affix; nail to

īnflammō (1) set on fire, kindle; inflame, excite

īnflectō, ere, ēxī, exus bend, bow, curb; change, affect, alter

īnfrēnus, a, um unbridled

īnfundō, ere, fūdī, fūsus pour in, pour upon; pour out, throw

ingeminō (1) redouble, repeat, reiterate

ingemō, ere, uī, — groan over, sigh at, lament, bewail

ingēns, entis huge, vast, enormous; extraordinary

ingredior, ī, gressus advance, go forward; undertake

inhiō (1) gape, gaze, gaze at

inhospitus, a, um inhospitable

inhumātus, a, um unburied

inimīcus, a, um hostile, unfriendly, hateful; damaging

inīquus, a, um uneven; unequal; hurtful

iniūria, ae *f.* injustice, wrong; harsh treatment

inlābor, ī, lapsus glide in; flow in, penetrate

inlīdō, ere, sī, sus dash against, push against

inlūdō, ere, sī, sus mock, ridicule

innectō, ere, nexuī, nexus twist, entangle, weave; bind; contrive

innō (1) swim in, float upon; sail, navigate

innūptus, a, um unmarried; a virgin

inopīnus, a, um unexpected

inops, opis helpless, weak

inquit says, said

inreparābilis, e irreparable, irretrievable

inrītō (1) incite, excite, provoke

inrumpō, ere, rūpī, ruptus break in, burst into

inruō, ere, uī, — rush in, invade

īnsānia, ae *f.* madness, folly

īnsānus, a, um insane, mad; outrageous, excessive

īnscrībō, ere, īpsī, īptus inscribe; mark

īnsequor, ī, cūtus follow after, come next; proceed, go on

īnsidiae, ārum *f. pl.* snare, trap; artifice

īnsīgnis, e distinguished, remarkable, prominent

īnsinuō (1) creep in; penetrate, enter

īnsomnium, (i)ī *n.* dream

īnsonō, āre, uī, — resound; crack

īnspiciō, ere, spexī, spectus look into, inspect; examine

īnspīrō (1) blow upon, inspire; instill

īnstar *n. indecl.* image, likeness, in the form of

īnstaurō (1) establish, ordain; renew; celebrate; refresh

īnstituō, ere, uī, ūtus put in place, fix, set; establish

īnstō, āre, stitī, — stand upon, take a position; press on, pursue

īnstruō, ēre, ūxī, ūctus draw up, array; prepare, equip

īnsuētus, a, um unaccustomed, unused

īnsula, ae *f.* island

īnsum, esse, fuī, — be in, be upon

īnsuper *adv.* above, on top, overhead; besides

īnsuperābilis, e insurmountable, invincible

īnsurgō, ere, rēxī, rēctus rise up, pull (with oars)

intāctus, a, um untouched, undefiled

intendō, ere, dī, tus stretch out, extend; increase

intentō (1) aim, direct, wield

intentus, a, um attentive, intent, waiting, eager

inter *prep.* between, among (+*acc.*)

intereā *adv.* meanwhile

interfor, ārī, ātus interrupt

interfundō, ere, fūdī, fūsus flow between; pour between

interimō, ere, ēmī, ēmptus take away; destroy, slay, kill

interior, ius inner, interior, middle

interpres, etis *m./f.* interpreter, explainer; mediator

interrumpō, ere, rūpī, ruptus break off, interrupt, break off

intexō, ere, texuī, textus weave in, interweave

intimus, a, um innermost, deepest, intimate

intonō, āre, uī, ātus thunder; resound, rattle; cry out

intorqueō, ēre, torsī, tortus twist, wind about, wrench; hurl

intrā *prep.* within, inside (+*acc.*)

intractābilis, e unmanageable, intractable

intrō (1) go into, enter; penetrate

intus *adv.* inside, within, closer

inultus, a, um unavenged

inūtilis, e useless, inexpedient

invādō, ere, vāsī, vāsus enter; assault, attack, invade

invalidus, a, um infirm, impotent, weak

invehō, ere, vexī, vectus carry in; ride into; drive over

inveniō, īre, vēnī, ventus find, meet with; discover

invictus, a, um unconquered, unsubdued; inexorable

invideō, ēre, vīdī, vīsus look askance at, envy; hinder, prevent

invidia, ae *f.* envy, grudge, jealousy

invīsō, ere, vīsī, vīsus look after, visit

invīsus, a, um hated, hateful, detested

invītus, a, um unwilling, reluctant

invius, a, um impassable, insuperable; inaccessible

involvō, ere, volvī, volūtus roll; cover, overwhelm; wrap, enfold, envelop

ipse, ipsa, ipsum himself, herself, itself

īra, ae *f.* anger, fury, hate

Īris, (id)is *f.* goddess of rainbow, also a messenger

is, ea, id he, she it; this, that

iste, ista, istud that (of yours) – often contemptuous

ita *adv.* thus, as follows, in that way

Ītalia, ae *f.* Italy

Ītalus, a, um of Italy, Italian

iter, itineris *n.* journey, passage, march, route, course

iterum *adv.* again, a second time, once more

iuba, ae *f.* mane; crest

iubar, aris *n.* radiance, light, splendor

iubeō, ēre, iussī, iussus order, tell, command

iūdicium, (i)ī *n.* judgment, sentence

iugālis, e yoked together; matrimonial; team (*noun*)

iugō (1) marry, bind

iugum, ī *n.* yoke, collar; summit, ridge; bonds

Iūlius, (i)ī *m.* Julius Caesar; Augustus Caesar

Iūlus, (i)ī *m.* another name for Ascanius

iungō (1) unite, join

iungō, ere, iūnxī, iūnctus join, unite, connect

Iūnō, ōnis *f.* goddess of marriage; wife of Jupiter

Iuppiter, Iovis *m.* Jupiter, king of the gods

iūrō (1) swear, take an oath; swear

iūs, iūris *n.* right, justice, duty

iussus, ūs *m.* order, command, decree

iūstus, a, um just, righteous; fair

Iūturna, ae *f.* sister of Turnus

iuvenālis, e youthful, juvenile

iuvencus, ī *m.* young bullock

iuvenis, e young, youthful; young person (*noun*)

iuventa, ae *f.* youth

iuventūs, ūtis *f.* youth; the young, young people

iuvō, āre, iūvī, iūtus help, aid, assist, serve; delight

iuxtā *prep. + adv.* near to, next to (+*acc*); in like manner

K

Karthāgō, inis *f.* Carthage, an ancient city in N. Africa

L

labefaciō, ere, fēcī, factus shake, loosen

labō (1) totter, waver, shake

labor, ōris *m.* labor, toil, exertion; suffering, hardship

lābor, ī, lapsus slip, glide, slide, move; sink, fall

lacrima, ae *f.* tear

lacrimō (1) shed tears, weep

lacus, ūs *m.* opening, lake

laedō, ere, laesī, laesus injure, hurt, wound, damage; insult

laena, ae *f.* mantle, shawl, cloak

laetitia, ae *f.* joy, happiness

laetor, ārī, ātus rejoice, exult

laetus, a, um joyous, happy, delighted; pleasant, grateful

laevus, a, um left; unfavorable

lambō, ere, ī lick, touch

lāmentābilis, e mournful, lamentable

lāmentum, ī *n.* wailing, moaning, weeping, lamentation

lampas, adis *f.* light, torch, lamp

languidus, a, um languid, dull, sluggish; faint, feeble

Lāöcoön, ontis *m.* Trojan priest of Apollo

lapis, idis *m.* stone

lapsō (1) slip

lapsus, ūs *m.* rolling, gliding; sinking

largior, īrī, ītus give bountifully, bestow, impart

largus, a, um abundant, copious, plentiful; flood

lassus, a, um faint, weary, tired

latebra, ae *f.* hiding-place, retreat

lateō, ēre, latuī, — lie hidden, be concealed; keep out of sight, escape notice

latex, icis *m.* liquid, water

Latīnī, ōrum *m. pl.* the people of Latium

Latīnus, a, um Latin, of Latium

Latīnus, ī *m.* king of Latium, father of Lavinia

Latium, (i)ī *n.* district in Italy south of the Tiber

Lātōna, ae *f.* mother of Diana and Apollo

lātus, a, um broad, wide, extensive

latus, eris *n.* side, flank

laudō (1) praise, honor, extol

Laurēns, entis of Laurentum, a town in Latium

laurus, ī *f.* bay tree, laurel tree

laus, laudis *f.* praise, commendation, glory, fame

Lausus, ī *m.* son of Mezentius (Turnus' Etruscan ally)

Lāvīnia, ae *f.* daughter of Latinus and Amata

Lāvīnium, (i)ī *n.* town in Latium

Lāvīnius, a, um of Lavinium

laxō (1) extend; open, loose, release; relieve, free

laxus, a, um loose, open roomy; yielding

lēgifer, fera, ferum law-giving

legō, ere, lēgī, lēctus gather, collect, choose, pick; survey

Lēnaeus, a, um of Bacchus, god of wine

lēniō, īre, īvī, ītus soften, mollify, soothe; appease, pacify

lēnis, e soft, smooth, mild, gentle

lentus, a, um pliant, flexible; slow, lingering, lazy

leō, ōnis *m.* lion

lētālis, e deadly, fatal, mortal

lētum, ī *n.* death, annihilation

levis, e light, swift, quick

lēvis, e smooth

levō (1) lift, raise, elevate

lēx, lēgis *f.* law, precept, regulation, principle

lībō (1) taste, sip; pour out, offer as a libation

lībrō (1) poise, balance; brandish

Liburnī, ōrum *m. pl.* people of northern Illyria

Libya, ae *f.* region of N. Africa

Libycus, a, um Libyan, of Libya

licet, ēre, licuit, licitus it is permitted, it is allowed

lignum, ī *n.* wood, firewood, timber

ligō (1) tie, bind

līlium, (i)ī *n.* lily

limbus, ī *m.* border, hem, edge, fringe

līmen, inis *n.* threshold, door, doorway; house, dwelling

līmes, itis *m.* path, passage, road; boundary, limit

lingua, ae *f.* tongue, language

linquō, ere, līquī, lictus go away, leave, depart from, abandon

liquēns, entis flowing, liquid

liquidus, a, um fluid, liquid; clear, bright, transparent

litō (1) make an acceptable sacrifice

lītus, ōris *n.* seashore, beach

lituus, ī *m.* crooked staff; trumpet, cornet

locō (1) place, put, lay; establish

locus, ī *m.* place, spot; position

Longa Alba Longa (*see* **Alba**)

longaevus, a, um aged, ancient

longē *adv.* far, far off; for a long period

longus, a, um long, extended

loquor, ī, locūtus speak, talk, say, tell; declare

lōrīca, ae *f.* coat of mail, leather cuirass

lōrum, ī *n.* leather thong; reins (*pl.*)

lūbricus, a, um slippery, slimy

Lūcifer, ferī *m.* morning star

luctor, ārī, ātus wrestle, struggle, strive, contend

lūctus, ūs *m.* sorrow, mourning, grief

lūcus, ī *m.* sacred grove

lūdibrium, (i)ī *n.* plaything, sport

lūdō, ere, lūsī, lūsus play; mock

lūmen, inis *n.* light; eyes (*pl.*)

lūna, ae *f.* moon

lūnātus, a, um half-moon shaped, crescent-shaped

luō, ere, luī, — loose, wash away; atone for, expiate

lupa, ae *f.* she-wolf

lūstrō (1) review, observe, examine; illuminate

lūstrum, ī *n.* period of five years; wood, forest wilderness

lūx, lūcis *f.* light, brightness; stars (*pl.*)

lūxus, ūs *m.* excess, indulgence, luxury; splendor, magnificence

Lyaeus, ī *m.* Greek name for Bacchus

Lycia, ae *f.* region in southwestern Asia Minor

Lycius, a, um of Lycia

Lycus, ī *m.* friend of Aeneas

Lȳdius, a, um of Lydia

lympha, ae *f.* water, clear water, spring water

lynx, lyncis *m./f.* lynx

M

Machāōn, onis *m.* one of the Greek fighters at Troy

māchina, ae *f.* machine, engine; device

mactō (1) honor, glorify, extol; kill, slaughter; offer, sacrifice

macula, ae *f.* spot, mark, stain; blot

maculōsus, a, um spotted, speckled

madeō, ēre, uī, — be wet, drip, flow

Maeonius, a, um of Maeonia, a province of Lydia; Lydian

maereō, ēre, uī, — mourn, grieve, lament

maeror, ōris, *m.* mourning, sadness, grief

maestus, a, um sorrowful, dejected, despondent

māgālia, ium *n. pl.* huts

mage (magis) more

magister, trī *m.* master; pilot; captain

magistrātus, ūs *m.* magistrate, public official

magnanimus, a, um great, high-minded

magnus, a, um large, great, huge, mighty; important

Maia, ae *f.* Mercury's mother, daughter of Atlas

māiestās, ātis *f.* greatness, majesty

mālō, malle, māluī, — prefer, rather

malus, a, um evil, wicked, bad; hostile

mamma, ae *f.* breast

mandātum, ī *n.* order, command, charge

mandō (1) entrust, deliver; order, command

mandō, ere, mandī, mansus chew, eat

maneō, ēre, mānsī, mānsus remain, stay

mānēs, ium *m. pl.* departed spirit, ghost, shade

manifestus, a, um clear, plain, apparent

manus, ūs *f.* hand; band, troop; handiwork

Marcellus, ī *m.* 1. Roman war hero 2. Son of Octavia

mare, is *n.* sea

marītus, ī *m.* husband, married man; suitor

marmor, oris *n.* marble

marmoreus, a, um of marble, marble

Marpēsius, a, um of Marpesia, a mountain in Paros

Mārs, Mārtis *m.* god of war

Massȳli, ōrum *m. pl.* the Massylians, a people of N. Africa

māter, tris *f.* mother; native land

māternus, a, um maternal

mātūrō (1) hasten, hurry

Maurūsius, a, um Moorish

Māvors, rtis *m.* Mars

Māvortius, a, um of Mars; warlike

meātus, ūs *m.* motion, movement

meditor, ārī, ātus consider, meditate, contemplate

medius, a, um the middle of, middle

medulla, ae *f.* marrow

mel, mellis *n.* honey

melior, ius better

membrum, ī *n.* limb, member; bodies (*pl.*)

meminī, isse remember, recollect

Memnōn, onis *m.* king of Ethiopians, son of Tithonus and Aurora

memor, oris mindful, remembering

memorābilis, e memorable, remarkable

memorō (1) mention, recount, speak of, tell; address

Menelāus, ī *m.* king of Sparta, Helen's husband

mēns, mentis *f.* mind, intellect; memory; feeling; heart

mēnsa, ae *f.* table; meal

mēnsis, is *m.* month

mentior, īrī, ītus lie, cheat, deceive, pretend; lie about

mentum, ī *n.* chin

mercor, ārī, ātus trade, purchase, buy

Mercurius, iī, *m.* messenger of the gods; son of Jupiter and Maia

mereō, ēre, uī, itus deserve, merit, be entitled to

mereor, ērī, itus deserve, merit, be entitled to

meritum, ī *n.* merit, service, kindness, benefit

meritus, a, um deserving, proper

mēta, ae *f.* end, boundary, limit; goal, turning post

metallum, ī *n.* metal

metuō, ere, uī, ūtus fear, be afraid

metus, ūs, *m.* fear, dread, apprehension

meus, a, um my, mine

micō, āre, uī, — gleam, glitter, flash; shake, tremble

migrō (1) depart, remove, migrate, go away

mīles, itis *m.* soldier

mīlia, ium *n. pl.* thousands

mīlle one thousand

minae, ārum *f. pl.* threats; pinnacles

Minerva, ae *f.* Roman name for Athena, goddess of household crafts

ministrō (1) attend, serve; provide, furnish

Mīnōius, a, um Minoan, of Minos (king of Crete)

minor, ārī, ātus project; threaten, menace

Mīnōtaurus, ī *m.* the Minotaur (half man, half bull)

minus *adv.* less

mīrābilis, e wonderful, marvelous, amazing

mīror, ārī, ātus wonder, marvel at, be astonished

mīrus, a, um wonderful, marvelous, astonishing

misceō, ēre, miscuī, mixtus mix, mingle, inter-mingle

Mīsēnus, ī *m.* friend of Aeneas, a trumpeter

miser, era, erum wretched, miserable, poor, sad

miserābilis, e miserable, pitiable

misereor, ērī, itus feel pity, have compassion

miseror, ārī, ātus lament, commiserate; pity

missilis, e able to be thrown; javelin, dart (*noun*)

mītēscō, ere grow mild, be tamed, be civilized

mitra, ae *f.* headband

mittō, ere mīsī, missus send, let go; throw; dismiss

Mnēstheus, eī *m.* friend of Aeneas

mōbilitās, ātis *f.* activity, mobility

modo *adv.* merely, only; just now, lately

modus, ī *m.* measure; way, manner; method

moenia, iūm *n. pl.* walls, ramparts; walled city

mōlēs, is *f.* mass, weight; greatness; difficulty, labor, trouble

mōlior, īrī, ītus exert, strive toil; build; rouse

molliō, īre, īvī, ītus soften, soothe; tame, restrain

mollis, e yielding, soft, tender, gentle

moneō, ēre, uī, itus advise, warn, admonish

monimentum (monumentum), ī *n.* reminder, memorial

monitus, ūs *m.* warning, reminding, admonition

mōns, montis *m.* mountain, hill; mass, heap

monstrō (1) point out, exhibit, indicate, inform; urge, advise

monstrum, ī *n.* divine omen, portent; monster, a horrible sight

mora, ae *f.* delay, procrastination; obstruction, hindrance

moribundus, a, um dying, at the point of death

morior, ī, mortuus die, expire; decay, wither

moror, ārī, ātus delay, stay, remain, linger

mors, mortis *f.* death

morsus, ūs *m.* bite, biting

mortālis, e mortal, transient

mōs, ōris *m.* practice, custom, habit; institution

mōtus, ūs *m.* movement, motion; moved

moveō, ēre, mōvī, mōtus move, remove, shake; excite, arouse, agitate

mox *adv.* soon, afterwards

mūgītus, ūs *m.* bellowing, lowing, mooing

mulceō, ēre, mulsī, mulsus soothe, soften, caress, flatter

multiplex, icis manifold, far more; varied

multus, a, um much; many (*pl.*); great, high, abundant

mūniō, īre, īvī, ītus fortify, build; guard, secure

mūnus, eris *n.* service, office; burial

mūrālis, e of a wall, mural

mūrex, icis *m.* purple dye; sharp stone

murmur, uris *n.* murmur, roar, growling, grumbling, crash

mūrus, ī *m.* wall, city wall

Mūsa, ae *f.* a muse, one of the nine Muses

mūtō (1) change, transform; exchange

Mycēnae, ārum *f. pl.* city of Argolis, where Agamemnon ruled

Myrmidones, um *m. pl.* Myrmidons, people of Thessaly

N

nam *conj.* for

namque *conj.* for

nārrō (1) tell, relate, make known; describe, mention

nāscor, ī, nātus be born, begin life; proceed

nāta, ae *f.* daughter

natō (1) swim, float

nātus, a, um born, made, destined, intended; a son

nauta, ae *m.* sailor, mariner

nāvigō (1) sail

nāvis, is *f.* ship

nē *adv.+ conj.* not; do not

-ne *(enclitic introducing a yes or no question)*

nebula, ae *f.* mist, vapor, fog, smoke

nec *adv.+ conj.* and not, also not; neither...nor

necdum *adv.+ conj.* nor yet, and not yet

nectar, aris *n.* nectar, drink of the gods; honey

nectō, ere, nexuī, nexus bind, tie, fasten; join

nefandus, a, um unspeakable, heinous, abominable

nefās *n. indecl.* sin, crime, wickedness

negō (1) deny, say...not, refuse

nemus, oris *n.* wood, grove, forest

Neoptolemus, ī *m.* Pyrrhus, son of Achilles

nepōs, ōtis *m.* grandson, descendant

Neptūnus, ī *m.* Neptune, god of the sea

neque *(same as* **nec***)*

nēquīquam *adv.* in vain, without reason

nesciō, īre, īvī, — not know, be ignorant

nescius, a, um ignorant, unaware

neu, nēve *adv.* and not, and that not, lest

nī *adv.+ conj.* if not, unless, that not

niger, gra, grum black, dark

nigrāns, ntis black, dark

nihil, nīl *n. indecl.* nothing

nimbus, ī *m.* rain storm, black cloud; cloud

nimium *adv.* too much, too; greatly

niteō, ēre, uī, — shine, glitter

nitidus, a, um shining, glittering, bright

nītor, ī, nīxus lean, support oneself; strive; rely

niveus, a, um snowy

nix, nivis *f.* snow; white hair

nō (1) swim, float; fly, sail

nocturnus, a, um nocturnal, by night

nōdō (1) tie in a knot

nōdus, ī *m.* knot; impediment

Nomas, adis *m.* tribe of North Africa

nōmen, inis *n.* name; title

nōn *adv.* not, by no means

nōndum *adv.* not yet

nōs we, us

nōscō, ere, nōvī, nōtus know, learn

noster, tra, trum our; ours

nōtus, a, um known, famous, customary

Notus, ī *m.* south wind; the winds

novem nine

novō (1) make new, renew, renovate

novus, a, um new, young, fresh; novel, last

nox, noctis *f.* night; death

noxa, ae *f.* hurt, harm, injury

nūbēs, is *f.* cloud, mist, vapor

nūbila, ōrum *n. pl.* clouds

nūdō (1) lay bare, expose, uncover

nūdus, a, um naked, bare, unclothed; destitute

nūllus, a, um no, none; worthless; no one

num (interrogative particle expecting a no answer)

nūmen, inis *n.* divinity, divine, power; a god or goddess

numerus, ī *m.* number, quantity

Numidae, ārum *m. pl.* Numidians, a people of North Africa

numquam *adv.* never

nunc *adv.* now

nuntia, ae *f.* female messenger

nuntiō (1) announce, declare, report

nuntius, (i)ī *m.* messenger, reporter; message, report, command

nurus, ūs *f.* daughter-in-law

nusquam *adv.* nowhere, in no place

nūtrīmentum, ī *n.* fuel, nourishment

nūtrīx, īcis *f.* nurse, wet-nurse

nympha, ae *f.* nymph

O

ō O! oh!

ob *prep.* on account of, because of (+*acc.*)

obeō, īre, īvī, itus go, go to meet; travel; engage in; surround

obiciō, ere, iēcī, iectus offer, present

obiectō (1) oppose; expose, endanger

obiectus, ūs *m.* opposition; opposing

obitus, ūs *m.* setting; downfall, ruin, death

oblīvīscor, ī, ītus forget

obmūtēscō, ere, uī, — be silent; become silent

obnītor, ī, nixus struggle with, strain against

oborior, īrī, ortus arise, appear, spring up

obruō, ere, uī, utus overwhelm; sink, submerge

obscūrus, a, um dark, shady, obscure; unknown

observō (1) watch, note; guard, observe

obsideō, ēre, sēdī, sessus beset, besiege

obstipēscō, ere, uī, — become senseless, be struck dumb

obstō, āre, stitī, stātus oppose, stand in the way

obstruō, ere, ūxī, ūctus build up, block; stop, hinder, impede

obtestor, ārī, ātus call as a witness, appeal to, implore

obtūtus, ūs *m.* gaze, contemplation

obvertō, ere, tī, sus turn towards, face

obvius, a, um in the way, meeting; against, opposite

occāsus, ūs *m.* downfall, destruction; falling, setting

occidō, ere, cidī, cāsus fall, perish; end, die

occulō, ere, culuī, cultus cover, conceal

occultō (1) hide, conceal

occumbō, ere, cubuī, cubitus die

ōceanus, ī *m.* great sea, the ocean

ōcior, ius swifter

oculus, ī *m.* eye

ōdī, ōdisse hate, dislike

odium, (i)ī *n.* hatred, ill-will

odor, ōris *m.* smell, scent, odor

odōrus, a, um scented, fragrant

offerō, ferre, obtulī, oblātus present, offer, show

Oīleus, eī *m.* father of Ajax

oleō, ēre, uī, — smell, emit a smell

ōlim *adv.* once, formerly; one day

olle (*same as* **ille**)

Olympus, ī *m.* Mount Olympus, home of the gods

ōmen, inis *n.* omen, sign, portent

omnīnō *adv.* completely, entirely

omnipotēns, ntis almighty, omnipotent

omnis, e all, every, whole

onerō (1) load, burden, fill, weigh down

onus, eris *n.* load, burden

onustus, a, um loaded, burdened, laden

opācō (1) make shady, shade, provide shade

opācus, a, um shady, shaded; shady places (*pl.*)

operiō, īre, uī, ertus cover, cover over

opertum, ī *n.* secret place

opīmus, a, um rich; **spolia opima**, arms won by a general from a general

opperior, īrī, per(ī)tus wait, wait for, attend

oppetō, ere, īvī, ītus encounter; die

oppōnō, ere, posuī, positus oppose; expose

oppositus, a, um opposed, opposite

opprimō, ere, pressī, pressus press down, crush

ops, opis *f.* aid, help, assistance; means, wealth, resources (*pl.*)

optō (1) choose, prefer

opulentus, a, um wealthy, opulent

opus, eris *n.* work, labor toil; structure, artistic work

ōra, ae *f.* shore, coast; border, edge, rim

orbis, is *m.* circle; world; shield

Orcus, ī *m.* god of the underworld; the underworld

ordior, īrī, orsus begin, commence

ordō, inis *m.* row, line, series; line, rank; troop, company

Orēas, adis *f.* a mountain nymph

orgia, ōrum *n. pl.* secret rituals, night festival of Bacchus

Oriēns, entis *m.* dawn; east, the orient

orīgō, inis *f.* beginning, start, birth

Ōrīōn, ōnis *m.* a constellation

orior, īrī, ortus rise, appear; be born, originate; rise, come forth

ornus, ī *f.* ash-tree

ōrō (1) beg, plead; pray, beseech; speak

Orontēs, is *m.* friend of Aeneas

Orpheus, ī *m.* famous mythological musician

ortus, ūs *m.* rising; sunrise

ōs, ōris *n.* mouth; face, expression

osculum, ī *n.* kiss

ostendō, ere, dī, tus show, point out, display

ostentō (1) exhibit, show; hold up

ostium, (i)ī *n.* door; mouth, entrance; harbor

ostrum, ī *n.* purple

ōtium, (i)ī *n.* leisure, free time; rest, repose, quiet

ovō (1) exult, rejoice, triumph

P

pābulum, ī *n.* food, food for cattle, fodder

pacīscor, ī, pactus agree, stipulate; bind

Pallas, adis *f.* Greek goddess Athena

Pallās, antis *m.* ally of Aeneas, son of Evander

palleō, ēre, uī, — grow pale, pale, blanch

pallidus, a, um pale, colorless

palma, ae *f.* palm, flat hand; palm tree, palm

palūs, ūdis *f.* swamp, marsh

pandō, ere, pandī, passus spread out, extend; open, lay open

Paphos, ī *f.* city in Cyprus, center for the worship of Venus

pār, paris equal, even; well-balanced

Parcae, ārum *f. pl.* the Fates

parcō, ere, pepercī, parsūrus spare, use moderately; abstain, refrain (+*dat.*)

parēns, ntis *m./f.* parent

pāreō, ēre, uī, — appear, be visible; obey, submit, comply

pariō, ere, peperī, partus give birth, produce; create, accomplish

Paris, idis *m.* Helen's abductor; son of Priam

parō (1) prepare, arrange, make ready

pars, partis *f.* part, portion; side

partior, īrī, ītus share, distribute, divide

partus, ūs *m.* birth, delivery

parum *adv.* too little, insufficiently

parvulus, a, um very small, little; young

parvus, a, um small; short, brief

pāscō, ere, pāvī, pāstus feed, nourish; graze

Pāsiphaē, ēs *f.* wife of Minos and mother of the Minotaur

passim *adv.* spread out, scattered, in every direction

pāstor, ōris *m.* shepherd, herdsman

Patavium, (i)ī *n.* Patavium, the modern Padua

patefaciō, ere, fēcī, factus lay open, throw open; disclose

pateō, ēre, uī, — be open, stand open

pater, tris *m.* father, sire

patera, ae *f.* bowl, saucer

patēscō, ere, uī, — be opened; stretch out, extend

patior, ī, passus bear, support, suffer, endure, allow

patria, ae *f.* native land, own country; home

patrius, a, um fatherly; traditional

paucī, ae, a few, few

paulum *adv.* a little, somewhat

pavidus, a, um trembling, fearful, timid

pavor, ōris *m.* trembling, shaking, terror

pāx, pācis *f.* peace, reconciliation

pectus, oris *n.* breast, chest, heart

pecus, pecudis *f.* a herd of cattle, beast, sacrificial animals

pecus, oris *n.* cattle; drones; flock

pedes, itis *m.* footsoldier

pelagus, ī *n.* sea

Pēlīdēs, ae *m.* son of Peleus, Achilles

pellis, is *f.* hide, skin, pelt

pellō, ere, pepulī, pulsus beat, strike, knock; drive out

pelta, ae *f.* light shield, half-moon shaped shield, pelt

penātēs, ium *m. pl.* household gods, gods of the state

pendeō, ēre, pependī, — hang, be suspended; loiter

pendō, ere, pependī, pēnsus suspend, weigh; ponder, consider

penetrābilis, e penetrable, piercing

penetrālia, ium *n. pl.* inner rooms, inner parts

penetrālis, e inward, inner

penetrō (1) penetrate, enter; pierce

penitus *adv.* inwardly, deeply; thoroughly

penna, ae *f.* feather, plume; wings (*pl.*)

Penthesilēa, ae *f.* queen of the Amazons

peplum, ī *n.* robe, mantle

per *prep.* through, along; throughout, during; by means of (+*acc.*)

peragō, ere, ēgī, āctus thrust through, pierce; review; accomplish

peragrō (1) wander through, travel, pass through

percutiō, ere, cussī, cussus strike through, pierce, transfix; slay, kill

pereō, īre, iī, itus perish, pass away, be destroyed

pererrō (1) wander through, roam over; survey

perferō, ferre, tulī, lātus bring home; reach the mark; carry, bring; report; bear

perficiō, ere, fēcī, fectus accomplish, achieve; execute, complete

perfidus, a, um dishonest, treacherous, perfidious

perflō (1) blow over, blow through

perforō (1) bore through, pierce, perforate

perfundō, ere, fūdī, fūsus pour over, drench; scatter over, besprinkle

Pergama, ōrum *n. pl.* Troy

Pergameus, a, um Trojan

pergō, ere, perrēxī, perrēctus proceed, go on, hasten

perhibeō, ēre, uī, itus bring forward; say, assert; call, name

perīculum, ī *n.* danger, peril, risk

perimō, ere, ēmī, ēmptus annihilate, destroy, prevent

Periphās, antis *m.* a Greek leader

perlābor, ī, lapsus slip through, glide over

perlegō, ere, lēgī, lēctus examine thoroughly, survey, peruse

permisceō, ēre, miscuī, mixtus mix together, mix thoroughly; mingle

permittō, ere, mīsī, missus hand over, entrust, surrender; allow

pernīx, īcis nimble, swift; persistent

perpetuus, a, um continuous, unbroken; forever

perrumpō, ere, rūpī, ruptus break through, force a way through

persentiō, īre, sēnsī, sēnsus feel deeply; perceive clearly

persolvō, ere, solvī, solūtus unravel, solve; render thanks; fulfill

personō, āre, uī, itus resound, reecho

pertaedet, ēre, taesum it wearies, disgusts, makes sick

pertemptō (1) prove thoroughly, test; try severely, overwhelm

perterritus, a, um terrified

perveniō, īre, vēnī, ventus reach, arrive; attain

pēs, pedis *m.* foot; sheet (nautical term)

pestis, is *f.* destruction, ruin, plague; curse, bane

petō, ere, īvī, ītus seek, aim at; attack; scan

phalanx, angis *f.* phalanx, compact armed formation, battalion

pharetra, ae, *f.* quiver

Phoebēus, a, um of Phoebus (Apollo)

Phoebus, ī *m.* Apollo

Phoenīcēs, um *m. pl.* Phoenicians

Phoenissus, a, um of Phoenicia; Dido (*noun*)

Phoenix, īcis *m.* Greek leader

Phryges, um *m. pl.* Trojans, Phrygians

Phrygius, a, um Phrygian, Trojan

Phthīa, ae *f.* district of Thessaly

piāculum, ī *n.* offering, sacrifice; remedy

picea, ae *f.* pitch-pine, pine

pictūra, ae *f.* painting, picture

pietās, ātis *f.* devotion, loyalty, dutiful conduct, sense of duty

piget, ēre, piguit it irks, pains, grieves

pīneus, a, um piney, pine

pingō, ere, pinxī, pictus paint, represent, depict

pinguis, e fat, juicy

pīnifer, era, erum pine-bearing

pinna, ae *f.* (*var. of* **penna**) feather, plume; wings (*pl.*)

piscōsus, a, um full of fish

pius, a, um devoted, dutiful, devout, conscientious

placeō, ēre, uī, itus please, give pleasure; (*impersonal*) it is agreed

placidus, a, um calm, gentle, quiet

plācō (1) soothe, assuage, appease, reconcile

plāga, ae *f.* region; net, snare

plangor, ōris *m.* striking, beating

planta, ae *f.* sprout, shoot; sole, sole of the foot

plēnus, a, um full, filled

plūma, ae *f.* feather, plume

plūs, plūris more, in greater number

poena, ae *f.* penalty, punishment

Poenī, ōrum *m. pl.* Carthaginians

Poenus, a, um Punic, Carthaginian

Polītes, ae *m.* son of Priam

polliceor, ērī, itus promise, offer

Pollūx, ūcis *m.* half brother of Castor, son of Jupiter and Leda

polus, ī *m.* pole; sky, heavens

pondus, eris *n.* weight, consequence, load

pōne *adv.* behind

pōnō, ere, posuī, positus put, place; establish; lay down

pontus, ī *m.* sea

poples, itis *m.* knee

populō (1) lay waste, ravage; destroy, ruin, mutilate

populus, ī *m.* people, nation

porta, ae *f.* door, gate; avenue, entrance, outlet

porticus, ūs *f.* colonnade, arcade, gallery, portico

portō (1) carry, bear

portus, ūs *m.* port, harbor

poscō, ere, poposcī, — ask, request, beg; demand

possum, posse, potuī, — be able, can

post *prep. + adv.* after, behind (+*acc.*); afterwards

posterus, a, um following, next; after; last

posthabeō, ēre, uī, itus place after, esteem less

postis, is *m.* post, doorpost; door

postquam *adv.* after, when

potēns, entis powerful, mighty; ruling

potior, īrī, ītus acquire, take possession of, have, hold (+*abl.*)

potius *adv.* rather, preferable, more

praeceps, cipitis headlong, in haste; plummeting

praecipiō, ere, cēpī, ceptus obtain beforehand, anticipate; advise, admonish

praecipitō (1) throw down; rush, sink rapidly, drop

praecipuus, a, um special, chief, excellent, distinguished

praeclārus, a, um famous; bright, brilliant, excellent

praecordia, ōrum *n. pl.* breast, heart

praeda, ae *f.* plunder, pillage, booty, spoil

praeficiō, ere, fēcī, fectus put in charge, appoint

praefixus, a, um tipped, pointed

praemittō, ere, mīsī, missus send ahead

praemium, (i)ī *n.* reward; advantage; prize

praepes, etis of good omen, favorable; a bird of good omen; swift

praeruptus, a, um broken off, steep, rugged

praesaepe, is *n.* hive

praescius, a, um prescient, foreknowing

praesēns, entis present, in person; prompt, efficacious

praesentiō, īre, sēnsī, sēnsus feel beforehand, presage, perceive in advance

praesēpe (*same as* **praesaepe**)

praesideō, ēre, sēdī, sessus be in charge, guard, watch, preside

praestāns, antis superior, excellent, distinguished, extraordinary

praestō, āre, stitī, stitus stand out, be superior, it is better

praetendō, ere, tendī, tentus hold out, extend, present; simulate, pretend

praetereā *adv.* besides, moreover

praetereō, īre, iī, itus to go by, go past, pass by; go beyond, outstrip

praeterlābor, ī, lapsus glide by, flow by

praetexō, ere, uī, tus weave; cover, conceal

praevertō, ere, tī, — go before, outrun; anticipate, prevent

prāvus, a, um crooked, distorted, deformed; improper, wrong

precor, ārī, ātus ask, beg, entreat, request

premō, ere, pressī, pressus press, pursue; overpower; bury; conceal; restrain

pre(he)ndō, ere, dī, sus grasp, snatch, seize; hold, stop

pretium, (i)ī, *n.* price, value, worth

prex, precis *f.* prayer, request

Priamus, ī *m.* Priam, king of Troy

prīmus, a, um first; chief, excellent

prīnceps, cipis *m.* leader, chief, founder, originator

prīncipium, (i)ī *n.* beginning, origin

prior, prius former, previous, prior, first

prīscus, a, um ancient, former, of old

prīstinus, a, um early, original, pristine

priusquam *adv.* before

prō *prep.* for; before, on account of; instead of (+*abl.*)

probō (1) approve, commend; recommend, show; prove

prōcēdō, ere, cessī, cessus go forward, proceed; advance, elapse

procella, ae *f.* violent wind, storm

procul *adv.* in the distance, far, from afar

prōcumbō, ere, cubuī, cubitus fall forwards, fall prostrate

prōdeō, īre, iī, itus go forth, come forward; advance

prōdō, ere, didī, ditus produce, propagate; report; reveal; betray

prōdūcō, ere, dūxī, ductus lead forward; bring forth, produce

proelium, (i)ī *n.* battle, combat

proficīscor, ī, fectus set out, depart, march

profor, ārī, fātus speak out, speak

profugus, a, um fugitive; banished, exiled

profundus, a, um deep, profound; of the underworld, infernal

prōgeniēs, ēī *f.* descent, lineage, race, family; descendants

prōgignō, ere, genuī, genitus beget, bear, bring forth

prōgredior, ī, gressus go forward, advance; progress

prōlābor, ī, lapsus glide forward, slide along, slip

prōlēs, is *f.* offspring, children, descendants

prōmereor, ērī, eritus deserve, merit, earn, be worthy

prōmittō, ere, mīsī, missus promise, hold out, assure, expect

prōmō, ere, mpsī, mpsus take out, give out, produce

prōnuba, ae *f.* bride's attendant

prōnus, a, um bent over, leaning; rushing; prone

propāgō, inis *f.* offspring, descendant

properō (1) hurry, hasten, move quickly

propior, ius closer, nearer

proprius, a, um special, peculiar, individual; lasting

propter *prep.* on account of, because of (+*acc.*)

prōpugnāculum, ī *n.* rampart, fortress, protection

prōra, ae *f.* prow, bow

prōrumpō, ere, rūpī, ruptus break out, rush forth, attack, burst

prōsequor, ī, secūtus pursue, follow up, chase

Prōserpina, ae *f.* wife of Pluto and queen of the underworld

prōspectus, ūs *m.* view, prospect

prōspiciō, ere, spexī, spectus look forward, look out, look, see, discern

prōtendō, ere, dī, tus extend, reach out, lift

prōtinus *adv.* forward, onward; continuously, without pause

prōvehō, ere, vexī, vectus move along, advance, lead on, proceed

proximus, a, um nearest, closest; next

pūbēs, is *f.* young men; groin

pudor, ōris *m.* decency, modesty, propriety; shame

puella, ae *f.* girl

puer, erī *m.* boy

pugna, ae *f.* fight, battle

pugnō (1) fight, combat, contend

pugnus, ī *m.* fist

pulcher, chra, chrum beautiful, handsome; fine, noble

pulsō (1) strike, beat, hammer, batter

pulverulentus, a, um dusty, covered with dust

pulvis, eris *m.* dust, powder

Pūnicus, a, um Punic, Carthaginian

puppis, is *f.* stern, poop; ship

purpureus, a, um purple, dark red

putō (1) think, consider, regard; judge, believe

Pygmaliōn, ōnis *m.* Dido's brother

Pyrrhus, ī *m.* Achilles' son

Q

quā *adv.* where? how? in any way

quaerō, ere, sīvī, sītus seek, look for, ask for

quālis, e what sort?; of such a kind, such as

quam *adv.* how, how much; than

quamquam *adv.* although, however

quandō *adv.* when? since

quantum *adv.* as much as, so much as

quantus, a, um of what size, how much, as

quassō (1) shake violently; shatter, batter

quater *adv.* four times

-que and (*enclitic*)

queō, quīre, quīvī, quītus be able

quercus, ūs *f.* oak, oak tree

querēla, ae *f.* complaint, accusation

queror, ī, questus express grief, complain, lament

quī, quae, quod who, which; what; that

quia *conj.* because

quīcumque, quaecumque, quodcumque whoever, whatever, whosoever

quidem *adv.* indeed, in fact

quiēs, ētis *f.* rest, repose, peace

quiēscō, ere, quiēvī, quiētus rest, repose, keep quiet

quiētus, a, um at rest, inactive, in repose

quīn *conj.* why not?; but, indeed

quīnquāgintā fifty

quippe *adv.* of course, obviously; indeed

Quirīnus, ī *m.* another name for Romulus

quis, quid who? what?

quisquam, quaequam, quicquam any, anyone

quisque, quaeque, quidque whoever, whatever; each one, everyone

quisquis, quidquid whoever, whatever; everyone who

quō *adv.* where; at which time; because; why

quod *conj. + adv.* because; that, in that; wherefore

quondam *adv.* once, at some time, at one time; sometimes

quoniam *adv.* since, because, whereas

quoque *conj.* also, too

quot how many?

quotannīs *adv.* every year, annually, yearly

quotiēns *adv.* how often?; as often as

R

rabidus, a, um raving, mad, enraged; inspired

rabiēs, em *(acc.) f.* rage, madness, frenzy; anger, fury

radius, (i)ī *m.* staff, rod; a geometer's rod; beam, ray

rādīx, īcis *f.* root, foundation

rāmus, ī *m.* branch, bough, twig

rapidus, a, um fierce; rushing, swift

rapiō, ere, rapuī, raptus seize, snatch, tear, pluck; drive

raptō (1) snatch, drag, hurry away

rārus, a, um loose, with large mesh; scattered, dispersed

ratiō, ōnis *f.* reason; account, calculation; course, conduct

ratis, is *f.* raft, boat

raucus, a, um hoarse; ringing; hollow-sounding

rebellis, e insurgent, rebellious

recēdō, ere, cessī, cessus fall back, withdraw, recede

recēns, entis fresh, young, recent

recidīvus, a, um restored; falling back; rising again

recipiō, ere, cēpī, ceptus receive, take back; recover, rescue

reclūdō, ere, sī, sus open, disclose, reveal; draw

recondō, ere, condidī, conditus put back, put away; plunge

rēctus, a, um right, correct; direct, straight

recursō (1) return persistently, keep recurring

recutiō, ere, cussī, cussus shake again, shock

reddō, ere, reddidī, redditus drive back, restore; reply, answer

redeō, īre, iī, itus go back, return

redimō, ere, ēmī, ēmptus buy back, redeem, ransom; release

reditus, ūs *m.* return, returning; circuit

redoleō, ēre, uī, — emit scent, smell of, be redolent of; breathe, exhale

redūcō, ere, dūxī, ductus lead back, bring back

redux, ucis brought back, restored

refellō, ere, fellī, — disprove, refute, repel, expose

referō, ferre, tulī, lātus bring back, carry back; recall, speak, say

reflectō, ere, flexī, flexus bend back, turn back

refringō, ere, frēgī, frāctus break up, break open

refugiō, ere, fūgī, — flee back, escape, avoid

refulgeō, ēre, fulsī, — flash back, glitter, glisten

refundō, ere, fūdī, fūsus pour back, make flow back

rēgīna, ae *f.* queen

regiō, ōnis *f.* region, area; direction; boundary line

rēgius, a, um royal, regal, kingly

rēgnātor, ōris *m.* ruler, sovereign

rēgnō (1) rule, reign, govern

regnum, ī *n.* kingdom; royalty

regō, ere, rēxī, rēctus rule, control; direct, guide

rēiciō, ere, iēcī, iectus throw back, hurl back

relinquō, ere, līquī, lictus leave, abandon, relinquish

reliquiae, ārum *f. pl.* remainders, remnants

rēmigium, (i)ī *n.* rowing, oarage

remittō, ere, mīsī, missus send back, drive back; loosen, relax; give up

remordeō, ēre, dī, sus bite again; vex, torment

removeō, ēre, mōvī, mōtus move back, drive away, remove

remūgiō, īre bellow back; resound

rēmus, ī *m.* oar

Remus, ī *m.* Romulus's brother

renovō (1) renew, restore; repeat

reor, rērī, ratus think, believe, suppose

repellō, ere, reppulī, repulsus drive back, drive away, repel

rependō, ere, pendī, pēnsus ransom; repay; balance

reperiō, īre, repperī, repertus find again, find, discover

repertor, ōris *m.* discoverer, inventor

repetō, ere, īvī, ītus attack again; seek again, demand back; retake, recall

repleō, ēre, ēvī, ētus fill again, refill, fill up

repōnō, ere, posuī, positus put back, restore; stretch out; lay aside, store

reprimō, ere, pressī, pressus keep back, check, curb, restrain, refrain

requiēs, ētis *f.* rest, repose, respite

requīrō, ere, quīsīvī, quīsītus seek again, search for; demand; require

rēs, rēī *f.* thing, incident, matter; state; exploits, world (*pl.*)

reservō (1) keep back, save up, reserve

resīdō, ere, sēdī, — sit down, settle; subside

resignō (1) unseal, open; reveal

resistō, ere, restitī, — remain, continue; oppose, resist

resolvō, ere, solvī, solūtus loosen, release, relax; dispel

resonō (1) resound, ring

respiciō, ere, spexī, spectus look back, gaze at, look for

respondeō, ēre, spondī, spōnsus reply, respond, answer; correspond

respōnsum, ī *n.* reply, answer, response; advice

restō, āre, restitī, — withstand, resist, oppose; remain

resupīnus, a, um bent back, lying on the back

resurgō, ere, surrēxī, surrēctus rise again, appear again

rēte, is *n.* net

retegō, ere, tēxī, tēctus uncover, bare, open; disclose, reveal

retorqueō, ēre, torsī, tortus twist back, turn back; change, alter

retractō (1) undertake anew; consider; withdraw

retrō *adv.* backward, back; formerly

revellō, ere, vellī, vulsus pull away, tear off; violate

revertō, ere, tī, sus turn back, return

revīsō, ere look back; revisit

revocō (1) recall, call again

revolvō, ere, volvī, volūtus revolve, turn again; unroll, repeat; return

rēx, rēgis *m.* king

Rhēsus, ī *m.* Thracian leader

rīdeō, ēre, rīsī, rīsus laugh; ridicule

rigeō, ēre be stiff, stiffen; bristle, harden

rīma, ae *f.* crack, fissure

rīpa, ae *f.* bank, shore

rīte *adv.* solemnly, ceremonially; rightly, fitly

rītus, ūs *m.* ceremony, rite

rōbur, ōris *n.* hardwood, oak; tree trunk; oak tree; strength

rogus, ī *m.* funeral pyre

Rōma, ae *f.* Rome

Rōmānus, a, um Roman

Rōmulus, a, um of Romulus

Rōmulus, ī *m.* first king and founder of Rome

rōscidus, a, um wet with dew, dewy; moistened

roseus, a, um rose-colored, ruddy

rota, ae *f.* wheel; chariot

rudēns, entis *m.* rope

ruīna, ae *f.* fall, crash, ruin

rūmor, ōris *m.* rumor, report; murmur

rumpō, ere, rūpī, ruptus break, burst, rupture; break through

ruō, ruere, ruī, ru(i)tus rush, hurry; fall down, tumble

rūpēs, is *f.* rock, cliff

rūrsus *adv.* again, in turn

rūs, rūris *n.* the country, fields

Rutulī, ōrum *m. pl.* Rutulians, Turnus's tribe

S

Sabaeus, a, um Sabaean (Arabian region)

sacer, cra, crum holy, sacred

sacerdōs, ōtis *m./f.* priest, priestess

sacra, ōrum *n. pl.* sacrifices

sacrō (1) consecrate, dedicate, devote

saeculum, ī *n.* generation, age; a lifetime

saepe *adv.* often, frequently

saepiō, īre, saepsī, saeptus hedge in, enclose, encircle; surround; protect

saeviō, īre, iī, ītus rage, rave

saevus, a, um savage, fierce, ferocious; terrible

sagitta, ae *f.* arrow, shaft

sal, salis *n.* salt water, the sea

saltem *adv.* at least, at all events, anyhow

saltus, ūs, *m.* leap, leaping; forest, woodland

salum, ī *n.* the open sea, the deep

salūs, ūtis *f.* health, welfare, prosperity; greeting

Samos, ī *f.* island off Asia Minor

sānctus, a, um holy, sacred; revered

sanguineus, a, um bloody, blood-red

sanguis, inis *m.* blood; bloodshed, slaughter

saniēs, ēī *f.* gore, bloody matter

sānus, a, um whole, healthy, well; sober, sane

Sarpēdōn, onis *m.* ally of the Trojans, Lycian king

sat(is) *adv.* enough, sufficient, adequate

sator, ōris *m.* father, creator

Sāturnia, ae *f.* Juno (daughter of Saturn)

Sāturnius, a, um of Saturn, Saturnian

Sāturnus, ī *m.* Saturn, father of Jupiter, king of Latium

saucius, a, um wounded, hurt, injured

saxum, ī *n.* large stone, boulder, rock

scaena, ae *f.* stage, scene; theater; space

scandō, ere climb, rise, ascend

scelerātus, a, um polluted, profaned; wicked, impious

scelerō (1) pollute, defile, desecrate

scelus, eris *n.* wicked deed, crime, sin, wickedness

sceptrum, ī *n.* scepter; kingdom, rule, authority

scīlicet *adv.* to be sure, indeed

scindō, ere, scidī, scissus cut, tear, rend, split, divide

scintilla, ae *f.* spark, glimmer, trace

sciō, īre, īvī, ītus know, understand

scopulus, ī *m.* rock, cliff, crag, ledge

scūtum, ī *n.* shield, protection, defense

Scyllaeus, a, um of Scylla, the famous sea monster

Scȳrius, a, um of Scyros (an Aegean island)

sē himself, herself, itself, themselves

sēcessus, ūs *m.* separation; ravine, hiding-place; narrow bay

secō, āre, uī, sectus cut, reap, carve; operate, divide

sēcrētum, *n.* mystery, hidden thing, secret

secundus, a, um favorable; second

secūris, is *f.* ax, hatchet

sēcūrus, a, um carefree, composed; cheerful, serene

secus *adv.* otherwise, differently

sed *conj.* but

sedeō, ēre, sēdī, sessus sit; hold court

sēdēs, is *f.* seat, dwelling-place; foundation

sedīle, is *n.* seat, bench, stool, chair

sēditiō, ōnis *f.* insurrection, mutiny; dissension, quarrel

sēdūcō, ere, dūxī, ductus take apart, lead away; divide, part

sēgnis, e slow, tardy, slack; sluggish

sēmen, inis *n.* seed, beginning; cause

sēmianimis, e half-alive, half-dead

sēminex, necis half-dead

sēminō (1) sow; produce

sēmita, ae *f.* path, lane

sēmivir, virī half-man; effeminate, unmanly

semper *adv.* always, ever, continually

senātus, ūs *m.* senate

senecta, ae *f.* old age, senility

senex, senis old, aged

sēnī, ae, a six each

senior, ōris *m.* old man

sēnsus, ūs *m.* observation, feeling, sensation; way of thinking

sententia, ae *f.* opinion, judgment, decision

sentiō, īre, sēnsī, sēnsus perceive, note; understand

sentus, a, um thorny, rough

sepeliō, īre, īvī, pultus bury; place on a funeral pyre; destroy, suppress

septem seven

septemplex, plicis sevenfold

septēnī, ae, a seven each

sepulc(h)rum, ī *n.* burial place, tomb, grave

sequor, ī, secūtus follow, pursue; accompany

serēnō (1) calm, make clear

serēnus, a, um calm, clear

Serestus, ī *m.* friend of Aeneas

Sergestus, ī *m.* friend of Aeneas

sermō, ōnis *m.* speech, conversation; talk, report, rumor

serō, ere, sēvī, satus sire, produce

serō, ere, uī, tus engage; join, discuss

serpēns, entis *m.* snake, serpent

serpō, ere, psī, ptus crawl, creep; creep in

serta, ōrum *n. pl.* garlands, wreaths

serviō, īre, īvī, ītus serve, work for

servitium (i)ī *n.* slavery, bondage

servō (1) save, guard, keep

sēsē himself, herself, itself, themselves (*same as* se)

seu *conj.* or, or if; whether...or (*same as* **sive**)

sex six

sī *conj.* if, when

sībilus, ī *m.* hissing

Sibylla, ae *f.* Sibyl, prophetess

sīc *adv.* thus, in this way

siccō (1) dry, stanch

siccus, a, um dry; thirsty

Siculus, a, um of Sicily; Sicilian

sīdō, ere, (sēd)ī, — perch, settle, sit down

Sīdonius, a, um of Sidon

sīdus, eris *n.* constellation, group of stars; the sky, heaven

signum, ī *n.* sign, indication; standard; figure

silentium, (i)ī *n.* silence, stillness

sileō, ēre, uī, — be silent, be still; suppress

silex, icis *m. (f.)* flint, granite

silva, ae *f.* wood, forest

similis, e similar, like, resembling

Simoīs, entis *m.* river near Troy

simul *adv.* at the same time, simultaneously

simulācrum, ī *n.* likeness, image, statue

simulō (1) pretend, feign, simulate

sīn *conj.* but if

sine *prep.* without (+*abl.*)

singulī, ae, a one at a time, single; separate

sinō, ere, sīvī, situs allow, permit

Sinōn, ōnis *m.* the Greek who tricks the Trojans

sinuō (1) curve, bend; fold

sinus, ūs *m.* bay; fold; bosom

sistō, ere, stitī, status set, set up, fix, plant; present; halt, stay; lead

sitis, is *f.* thirst; drought

situs, ūs *m.* position, spot, place; neglect

sīve *conj.* whether; or if

sociō (1) associate; bind, unite

socius, (i)ī *m.* friend, comrade, ally

sōl, sōlis *m.* sun

sōlāmen, inis *n.* solace, consolation, comfort

soleō, ēre, itus be accustomed

solidus, a, um undivided, whole, complete; trustworthy

solium, (i)ī *n.* throne; seat

sollemnis, e solemn; sacred; accustomed

sollicitō (1) disturb, bother, trouble

sōlor, ārī, ātus console oneself for; cheer, comfort

solum, ī *n.* ground, base, foundation

sōlus, a, um alone, only, single, sole

solvō, ere, solvī, solūtus loosen, relax; release, unfurl; dispel, dismiss

somnus, ī *m.* sleep, slumber

sonipēs, pedis *m.* charger, steed

sonitus, ūs *m.* sound, noise, din

sonō, āre, uī, sonitus resound, make a noise; speak, express

sonōrus, a, um howling, roaring, resounding

sopor, ōris *m.* slumber, deep sleep

soror, ōris *f.* sister

sors, sortis *f.* fate, lot; prophecy; destiny, fortune

sortior, īrī, ītus cast lots, draw lots; share, divide; choose

spargō, ere, sī, sus scatter, sprinkle, strew

Spartānus, a, um Spartan

spatior, ārī, ātus walk, wander around

spatium, (i)ī *n.* space, room; level; path

speciēs, ēī *f.* sight, appearance; spectacle; resemblance

spectāculum, ī *n.* sight, spectacle

spectātor, ōris *m.* spectator

specula, ae *f.* lookout, watchtower

speculor, ārī, ātus watch, keep watch; observe

spēlunca, ae *f.* cave

spernō, ere, sprēvī, sprētus scorn, disdain; reject

spērō (1) hope, look for, expect

spēs, ēī *f.* hope

spīra, ae *f.* fold, coil

spīritus, ūs *m.* spirit, soul; breath

spīrō (1) breathe

spoliō (1) strip, uncover, bare; rob, plunder

spolium, (i)ī *n.* hide; arms stripped from an enemy; booty (*pl.*)

sponte *f.* freely, willingly (*abl. only*)

spūma, ae *f.* spray, froth, foam

spūmeus, a, um foamy

spūmō (1) foam, froth

spūmōsus, a, um foaming, foamy

squāleō, ēre, uī, — be filthy

squāmeus, a, um scaly

stabilis, e firm, steady, stable, fixed; firm, lasting

stabulum, ī *n.* stall, stable; lair

stāgnum, ī *n.* swamp, standing water

statiō, ōnis *f.* resting place; anchorage

statuō, ere, uī, ūtus set up, station; construct, build

stellātus, a, um studded; gleaming

sternō, ere, strāvī, strātus spread out; overthrow, level, flatten

Sthenelus, ī *m.* Diomedes' charioteer

stimulō (1) spur; prick, goad on

stimulus, ī *m.* spur

stīpes, itis *m.* trunk (of a tree)

stīpō (1) press, pack; accompany; fill, cram, stuff

stirps, pis *m./f.* stem; lineage

stō, stāre, stetī, status stand; be built; linger, remain

strātum, ī *n.* covering; bed, couch

strepitus, ūs *m.* din, clash, rustle, clatter

strīdeō, ēre, dī, — make a harsh noise, hiss

strīdor, ōris *m.* shrill sound, creak, grating, rattle

stringō, ere, strinxī, strictus graze, trim, strip

struō, ere, ūxī, ūctus place together, heap up; prepare, devise

studium, (i)ī *n.* desire, exertion, endeavor; pursuit

stupeō, ēre, uī, — be stunned, be amazed; wonder at

stuppeus, a, um hempen, made of hemp

Stygius, a, um of the Styx (river in the underworld)

Styx, Stygis *f.* river of the underworld

suādeō, ēre, sī, sus advise, exhort, urge, persuade

sub *prep.* under, beneath; at the foot of (*+abl.*); to, toward (*+acc.*)

subeō, īre, iī, itus go under, enter; come up, advance; support; follow

subiciō, ere, iēcī, iectus place under; set up, mount; ascribe

subigō, ere, ēgī, āctus drive on, propel; force

subitō *adv.* suddenly, immediately, at once

subitus, a, um sudden

sublīmis, e lofty, high, exalted; on high, lofty; eminent

sub(sum)mergō, ere, rsī, rsus dip, plunge under, sink

sub(sum)mittō, ere, mīsī, missus put down, lower; moderate; humble, yield

subnectō, ere, nex(u)ī, nexus tie under, fasten beneath

subnixus, a, um leaning on; supported by

subolēs, is *f.* child; offspring

subrīdeō, ēre, rīsī — smile

subrigō, ere, surrēxī, surrēctus lift, raise

subsīdō, ere, sēdī, sessus settle down, subside

subsistō, ere, stitī, — halt, take a stand, stop; oppose

subter *adv.* beneath, under

subtrahō, ere, trāxī, tractus withdraw; *pass.* fly beneath

subvolvō, ere, ī, volūtus roll up

succēdō, ere, cessī, cessus go below, enter; ascend; succeed; approach; take up

successus, ūs *m.* success

succidō, ere, succidī, — fall, fail; sink down

succingō, ere, nxī, nctus gird; equip

succumbō, ere, cubuī, cubitus yield to, fall under

succurrō, ere, currī, cursus help, relieve; succour

sufferō, sufferre, sustulī, sublātus submit to, endure, suffer

sufficiō, ere, fēcī, fectus suffuse, tinge; supply; be sufficient

suffundō, ere, fūdī, fūsus pour in; suffuse

sulcus, ī *m.* furrow; trench

sum, esse, fuī, futūrus be

summus, a, um uppermost, highest; loftiest, supreme

sūmō, ere, sumpsī, sumptus take, lay hold of, assume; undertake; inflict

super *adv. + prep.* above, over, on top of (*+acc.*)

superbus, a, um proud, arrogant, insolent

superēmineō, ēre surpass, tower over

superī, ōrum *m. pl.* the gods

superō (1) surpass, overcome, transcend; remain; excel, be superior

superstitiō, ōnis *f.* superstition, dread of the supernatural

supersum, esse, fuī, — survive; remain; suffice

superus, a, um upper, higher

supīnus, a, um lying on one's back

supplex, icis *m.* suppliant; *adj.* beseeching, entreating

suppliciter *adv.* humbly, suppliantly

supplicium, (i)ī *n.* punishment, penalty

suppōnō, ere, posuī, positus apply; put under

suprā *adv. + prep.* above, over (*+acc.*)

suprēmum *adv.* for the last time

sūra, ae *f.* calf; leg

surgō, ere, surrēxī, surrēctus rise, get up, stand up; ascend

suscipiō, ere, cēpī, ceptus take, catch, take up; have, get; undertake, undergo, be born

suspendō, ere, dī, sus hang, suspend

suspiciō, ere, spexī, spectus look up at, admire; suspect

suspīrō (1) sigh

suus, a, um his, her, its, their

Sȳchaeus, ī *m.* Dido's husband (slain by Pygmalion)

Syrtis, is *f.* Syrtis (shallow sandy bays on the coast of Africa)

T

tābeō, ēre be drenched

tabula, ae *f.* board, plank

taceō, ēre, uī, itus be silent, say nothing

tacitus, a, um secret, unmentioned, silent

taeda, ae *f.* torch; nuptial torch

tālāria, ium *n. pl.* sandals

tālis, e such, of such a kind

tam *adv.* so, so very

tamen *adv.* however, nevertheless, still

tandem *adv.* at last, finally; pray now

tangō, ere, tetigī, tāctus touch; border on, reach

tantum *adv.* so much, so greatly

tantus, a, um so great, so much, such

Tartara, ōrum *n. pl.* Tartarus, the underworld

taurīnus, a, um a bull's; of a bull

taurus, ī *m.* bull; bullock

tēctum, ī *n.* house, dwelling; roof;

teg(i)men, inis *n.* covering, cover

tegō, ere, tēxī, tēctus cover, cover over, hide; shelter; dissemble, keep secret

tēla, ae *f.* texture, web; textile

tellūs, ūris *f.* earth, globe, land, ground; personified Earth

tēlum, ī *n.* spear, shaft, javelin; weapon

temperō (1) restrain oneself, abstain, keep from; soothe

tempestās, ātis *f.* storm, tempest; disturbance; multitude

templum, ī *n.* temple, sanctuary, shrine

temptō (1) try, attempt; tempt

tempus, oris *n.* time; occasion, opportunity

tenāx, ācis tenacious, griping, clinging

tendō, ere, tetendī, tentus stretch, extend; present; aim; exert, strive

tenebrōsus, a, um dark, gloomy

Tenedos, ī *f.* island near Troy

teneō, ēre, uī, tus hold, keep, have; occupy; hold back, detain; reach

tentōrium, (i)ī *n.* tent

tenuis, e slim, thin; little, slight; low

tenus *prep.* up to, as far as (+*abl.*)

ter *adv.* three times, thrice

terebrō (1) bore into, pierce

teres, etis smooth, polished

tergum, ī *n.* back, rear; hide, leather

tergus, oris *n.* hide, back

terminō (1) end; limit

ternī, ae, a triple

terō, ere, trīvī, trītus graze, touch; wear away, waste

terra, ae *f.* earth, land, soil; personified Earth

terreō, ēre, uī, itus frighten, terrify

terribilis, e dreadful, fearful

terrificō (1) terrify

territō (1) terrify, frighten

tertius, a, um third

testor, ārī, ātus call to witness; swear by

testūdō, inis *f.* tortoise shell; roof

tētē intensive form of **tē**

Teucer, crī *m.* early Trojan king

Teucrī, ōrum *m. pl.* Trojans

Teucria, ae *f.* Troy

thalamus, ī *m.* inner room, chamber; marriage bed

theātrum, ī *n.* theater

thēsaurus, ī *m.* treasure

Thēseus, ī *m.* king of Athens

Thessandrus, ī *m.* Greek warrior at Troy

Thoās, antis *m.* Greek warrior at Troy

Thrēicius, a, um Thracian, of Thrace

Threissa, ae *f.* Thracian; a Thracian woman

Thybris, idis *m.* Tiber River

Thȳias, adis *f.* Bacchant, Thyiad

Thymoetēs, ae *m.* a Trojan

thymum, ī *n.* thyme

Tiberīnus, a, um of the Tiber

Tiberīnus, ī *m.* god of the Tiber

tigris, idis *m* tigress, tiger

Timāvus, ī *m.* river in northeastern Italy

timeō, ēre, uī, — fear, be afraid of

timor, ōris *m.* fear, dread, anxiety

Tītān, ānis *m.* Titan, name given to the god of the sun

togātus, a, um wearing a toga

tollō, ere, sustulī, sublātus lift, raise; erect; extol, exalt

tonitrus, ūs *m.* thunder

tormentum, ī *n.* machine for hurling

torqueō, ēre, torsī, tortus twist, bend, turn

torreō, ēre, torruī, tostus roast

torus, ī *m.* sofa, couch, bed

torvus, a, um stern, grim

tot so many, such a number of

totidem just so many, just as many

totiēns *adv.* so often, as often

tōtus, a, um entire, all, whole

trabs, trabis *f.* beam, timber, rafter

tractābilis, e tangible, manageable, yielding, sympathetic

trahō, ere, trāxī, tractus draw, drag; lead; sweep along; spend, prolong; determine

trāiciō, ere, iēcī, iectus throw across; strike; pass through, penetrate

tranō (1) fly over; swim across

tranquillus, a, um calm, tranquil

transeō, īre, iī (īvī), itus go across, go over; pass by

transferō, ferre, tulī, lātus carry across; transfer

transfīgō, ere, fīxī, fīxus pierce

transmittō, ere, mīsī, missus send across; transfer

transverberō (1) transfix

tremefactus shaken

tremendus, a, um horrible, dreadful, terrible

tremescō, ere tremble, quake, shudder

tremō, ere, uī, — tremble, shake, quake

tremor, ōris *m.* trembling

trepidō (1) tremble, shake

trepidus, a, um restless, agitated, anxious

trēs, tria three

tridēns, entis with three teeth; trident

trietēricus, a, um biennial (triennial in Roman system)

trīginta thirty

Trīnacrius, a, um Sicilian

trīstis, e sad, sorrowful, dejected; dismal, gloomy

trisulcus, a, um three-forked

Trītōn, ōnis *m.* sea-god, son of Neptune

triumphus, ī *m.* triumph

Trivia, ae *f.* Hecate, underworld goddess

Trōia, ae *f.* Troy

Trōiānus, a, um Trojan

Trōilus, ī *m.* one of Priam's sons

Trōius, a, um Trojan

Trōs, Trōis *m.* a Trojan

trucīdō (1) kill, butcher

trūdō, ere, sī, sus push

truncus, ī *m.* body, trunk

trux, trucis harsh, fierce, wild

tū you

tueor, ērī, tūtus (tuitus) look at, behold, watch; keep in mind; care for, guard

tum *adv.* then, at that time, in those times; further

tumeō, ēre, uī, — swell, be swollen

tumidus, a, um swollen, tumid; puffing up

tumultus, ūs *m.* uproar, commotion, disturbance, tumult

tumulus, ī *m.* sepulchral mound, grave; heap of earth

tunc *adv.* then

tundō, ere, tutudī, tū(n)sus beat, strike, thump; pound, bruise; stun

turba, ae *f.* uproar, commotion; crowd, throng

turbidus, a, um confused, disordered; troubled, violent

turbō, inis *m.* whirlind, tornado

turbō (1) disturb, make an uproar, trouble

Turnus, ī *m.* leader of the Rutulians, Aeneas's enemy

turpis, e ugly; filthy, disgraceful

turris, is *f.* tower, citadel

tūs, tūris *n.* incense

tūtus, a, um safe, secure

tuus your

Tȳdīdēs, ae *m.* son of Tydeus, Diomedes

tyrannus, ī *m.* tyrant

Tyrius, a, um Tyrian, of Tyre

Tyros, ī *f.* Tyre, city in Phoenicia

Tyrrhēnus, a, um Tyrrhenian

U

ūber, eris *n.* breast, udder

ubi *adv.* where?; where, when

ubīque *adv.* everywhere, anywhere

ulcīscor, ī, ultus avenge

Ulixēs, is *m.* Ulysses (Odysseus)

ūllus, a, um any, any one

ulterior, ius farther, more remote

ultimus, a, um last; furthest

ultrā *adv.+ prep.* beyond, on the other side; more than (+*acc.*)

ultrō *adv.* on the other side, beyond

ululātus, ūs *m.* wailing, howling

ululō (1) howl, yell, wail

umbō, ōnis *m.* boss

umbra, ae *f.* shadow, shade

umbrifer, era, erum shade-giving

ūmectō (1) moisten, wet

ūmēns, entis moist, dewy, wet

umerus, ī *m.* shoulder, upper arm

ūmidus, a, um dewy, watery

umquam *adv.* ever

ūnā *adv.* at once, together, at the same time

ūnanimus, a, um sympathizing, agreeing

uncus, a, um hooked, crooked

unda, ae *f.* wave

unde *adv.* from which place, whence

undique *adv.* from all parts, on all sides, all around

undōsus, a, um billowy

unguis, is *m.* fingernail

unguō, ere, unxī, ūnctus smear, anoint

ūnus, a, um one, only, alone

urbs, urbis *f.* city

urgeō, ēre, ursī, — press, force, urge; drive

urna, ae *f.* urn

ūrō, ere, ussī, ustus burn

usquam *adv.* anywhere, any place

ūsus, ūs *m.* use

ut *conj.+ adv.* as, when; to, so that; that; as, when

uterque, utraque, utrumque each, either, each one; both (*pl.*)

uterus, ī *m.* womb; belly

uti (*same as* **ut**)

ūtor, ī, ūsus use, profit; spend; perform, practice (+*abl.*)

uxōrius, a, um uxorious, devoted to one's wife

V

vacca, ae *f.* cow; heifer

vacō (1) be free

vacuus, a, um empty, vacant, clear; free, free from

vādō, ere go, walk

vadum, ī *n.* shallow place, ford

vāgīna, ae *f.* sheath

vagor, ārī, ātus wander, roam; spread

valeō, ēre, uī, — be well, be strong; say goodbye

validus, a, um strong, powerful, robust

valles, is *f.* valley, vale

vānus, a, um empty, void; fruitless; false, deceptive

varius, a, um various, variegated; changing, variable; fickle

vastō (1) pillage

vastus, a, um unoccupied; vast, immense, huge

vātēs, is *m./f.* seer, prophet; prophetess

-ve *enclitic* or, or if you will

vehō, ere, vexī, vectus carry, bear; bring, usher in

vel *adv.* or, or indeed; certainly; *conj.* **vel...vel** either...or

vēlivolus, a, um sail-winged

vellō, ere, vulsī, vulsus tear, pluck

vēlō (1) cover, wrap

vēlōx, ōcis swift

vēlum, ī *n.* sail

velut *adv.* just as, even as, like

vēna, ae *f.* vein, artery; heart (*pl.*)

vēnābulum, ī *n.* hunting spear

vēnātrīx, īcis *f.* huntress

vendō, ere, didī, ditus sell

venēnum, ī *n.* poison; drug

venia, ae *f.* indulgence, kindness, favor; permission

veniō, īre, vēnī, ventus come, arrive; go

vēnor, ārī, ātus hunt

ventus, ī *m.* wind

Venus, eris *f.* goddess of Love, Aeneas's mother

verbum, ī *n.* word

vereor, ērī, itus fear

vērō *adv.* in fact, in truth, truly

verrō, ere, ī, versus sweep

versō (1) whirl, twist

vertex, icis *m.* whirlpool, vortex; peak, summit

vertō, ere, tī, sus turn, direct, change; twist; destroy

verū, ūs *n.* spit (*for cooking*)

vērum, ī *n.* reality, truth; *adv.* but

vērus, a, um true, real, actual, genuine

Vesper, eris *m.* the evening star

Vesta, ae *f.* goddess of the hearth

vester, tra, trum your

vestibulum, ī *n.* entrance

vestīgium (i)ī *n.* step, footprint, track; trace, mark, vestige

vestīgō (1) search, track

vestis, is *f.* clothing, attire, garments

vetō, āre, uī, itus forbid

vetus, eris old, aged

via, ae *f.* way, road, path; method, mode

vibrō (1) shake, brandish, wield; glimmer, gleam

vicissim *adv.* in turn

victor, ōris *m.* winner, victor, conqueror

victus, ūs *m.* food

videō, ēre, vīdī, vīsus see, perceive; understand; seem, appear (*passive*)

vigeō, ēre, uī, — thrive

vigil, ilis awake, alert; watchful, restless; guard (*noun*)

vīmen, inis *n.* twig, stem

vinciō, īre, vīnxī, vinctus bind, tie, fasten

vincō, ere, vīcī, victus conquer, overcome, defeat; banish

vinc(u)lum, ī *n.* chain, rope, fetter; bond

vindicō (1) claim; rescue

vīnum, ī *n.* wine

violō (1) injure, dishonor; violate

vir, virī *m.* man, male

vireō, ēre, uī be green, grow

virga, ae *f.* wand; branch, twig

virgō, inis *f.* young woman, virgin

viridis, e green

virtūs, ūtis *f.* strength, courage, excellence; character, virtue

vīs, vīs *f.* force, violence; strength (*pl.*)

vīscum, ī *n.* mistletoe

vīscus, eris *n.* flesh; organs

vīsum, ī *n.* appearance, sight

vīsus, ūs *m.* sight, vision; appearance

vīta, ae *f.* life

vītālis, e vital, of life

vitta, ae *f.* band, fillet, braid

vīvō, ere, vīxī, vīctus live, be alive; linger

vīvus, a, um alive, living

vix *adv.* scarcely, barely; just

vocō (1) call, name; invite; invoke

volātilis, e winged

volō, velle, voluī, — wish, want, desire

volō (1) fly

volucer, cris, cre winged, flying

volūmen, inis *n.* coil; fold

voluntās, ātis *f.* will, wish, choice, desire; purpose

volūtō (1) roll, turn; weigh, ponder, consider

volvō, ere, volvī, volūtus turn, roll; ordain, decree; glide

vorō (1) swallow

vōs you

vōsmet intensive form of **vōs**

vōtum, ī *n.* vow, solemn pledge; a votive offering

voveō, ēre, vōvī, vōtus vow

vōx, vōcis *f.* voice, cry, call; word, saying

vulgō (1) make known, spread abroad

vulgus, ī *n.* crowd, throng; rabble

vulnus, eris *n.* wound, injury

vultus, ūs *m.* face, appearance; expression

X

Xanthus, ī *m.* river near Troy

Z

Zephyrus, ī *m.* west wind

Graphic Latin Grammar* 1

1. REGULAR VERBS

In Latin the verb is especially important. It causes the subject either to act or to be acted upon. It expresses mood, voice, tense, person, and number. It includes four participles, the gerund, and the supine.

The present, imperfect, and the future indicative tenses, active and passive, are formed from the *present stem*, obtained by removing the -re from the present infinitive. The three perfect indicative active tenses are formed from the *perfect stem*, obtained by removing the -ī from the third principal part. The three perfect indicative passive tenses are formed from the fourth principal part, the entire *perfect passive participle*.

First Conjugation

PRINCIPAL PARTS OF LAUDŌ
laudō, Pres. Ind., Act., lst Sing.,   *I praise*
laudāre, Pres. Inf. Act.,   *to praise*
laudāvī, Perf. Ind. Act., 1st Sing.,   *I have praised, I praised*
laudātus, Perf. Pass. Part.,   *having been praised*

PARTICIPLES
Present Active: laudāns   *praising*
Perfect Passive: laudātus, -a, -um   *having been praised*
Future Active: laudātūrus, -a, -um   *being about to praise*
Gerundive: laudandus, -a, -um   *worthy to be praised*

INDICATIVE ACTIVE

Present		Perfect	
laudō	*I praise*	laudāvī	*I have praised*
laudās	*you...*	laudāvistī	*you have...*
laudat	*he praises*	laudāvit	*he has...*
laudāmus	*we praise*	laudāvimus	*we have...*
laudātis	*you...*	laudāvistis	*you have...*
laudant	*they...*	laudāvērunt	*they have...*
Imperfect		*Pluperfect*	
laudābam	*I was praising*	laudāveram	*I had praised*
laudābās	*you were...*	laudāverās	*you had...*
laudābat	*he was...*	laudāverat	*he had...*
laudābāmus	*we were...*	laudāverāmus	*we had...*
laudābātis	*you were...*	laudāverātis	*you had...*
laudābant	*they were...*	laudāverant	*they had...*
Future		*Future Perfect*	
laudābō	*I shall praise*	laudāverō	*I shall have praised*
laudābis	*you will...*	laudāveris	*you will have...*
laudābit	*he will...*	laudāverit	*he will have...*
laudābimus	*we will...*	laudāverimus	*we will have...*
laudābitis	*you will...*	laudāveritis	*you will have...*
laudābunt	*they will...*	laudāverint	*they will have...*

INFINITIVES
ACTIVE
Present: laudāre   *to praise*
Perfect: laudāvisse   *to have praised*
Future: laudātūrus esse   *to be about to praise*
PASSIVE
Present: laudārī   *to be praised*
Perfect: laudātus esse   *to have been praised*
Future: laudātum īrī (rare)   *to be about to be praised*

GERUND
Nominative: laudāre   *praising*
Genitive: laudandī   *of praising*
Dative: laudandō   *for praising*
Accusative: laudandum   *praising*
Ablative: laudandō   *by praising*

SUPINE
laudātum   *to praise*
laudātū   *to praise*

IMPERATIVE ACTIVE
PRESENT
Sing.: laudā   *praise*
Plur.: laudāte   *praise*

IMPERATIVE PASSIVE
PRESENT
Sing.: laudāre   *be praised*
Plur.: laudāminī   *be praised*

SUBJUNCTIVE ACTIVE[1]

Present	Perfect
laudem	laudāverim
laudēs	laudāverīs
laudet	laudāverit
laudēmus	laudāverīmus
laudētis	laudāverītus
laudent	laudāverint
Imperfect	*Pluperfect*
laudārem	laudāvissem
laudārēs	laudāvissēs
laudāret	laudāvisset
laudārēmus	laudāvissēmus
laudārētis	laudāvissētis
laudārent	laudāvissent

SUBJUNCTIVE PASSIVE

Present	Perfect	
lauder	laudātus, -a, -um	**sim**
laudēris	laudātus, -a, -um	**sīs**
laudētur	laudātus, -a, -um	**sit**
laudēmur	laudātī, -ae, -a	**sīmus**
laudēminī	laudātī, -ae, -a	**sītis**
laudentur	laudātī, -ae, -a	**sint**
Imperfect	*Pluperfect*	
laudārer	laudātus, -a, -um	**essem**
laudārēris	laudātus, -a, -um	**essēs**
laudārētur	laudātus, -a, -um	**esset**
laudārēmur	laudātī, -ae, -a	**essēmus**
laudārēminī	laudātī, -ae, -a	**essētis**
laudārentur	laudātī, -ae, -a	**essent**

[1]No meanings are given for the subjunctive because of the great variety of its uses. Each use calls for its own, special translation.

INDICATIVE PASSIVE

Present		Future		Pluperfect		
laudor	*I am (being) praised*	laudābor	*I shall be praised*	laudātus, -a, -um	**eram**	*I had been praised*
laudāris	*you are...*	laudāberis	*you will be...*	laudātus, -a, -um	**erās**	*you had been...*
laudātur	*he is...*	laudābitur	*he will be...*	laudātus, -a, -um	**erat**	*he had been...*
laudāmur	*we are...*	laudābimur	*we shall be...*	laudātī, -ae, -a	**erāmus**	*we had been...*
laudāminī	*you are...*	laudābiminī	*you will be...*	laudātī, -ae, -a	**erātis**	*you had been...*
laudantur	*they are...*	laudābuntur	*they will be...*	laudātī, -ae, -a	**erant**	*they had been...*
Imperfect		*Perfect*		*Future Perfect*		
laudābar	*I was being praised*	laudātus, -a, -um **sum**	*I have been praised*	laudātus, -a, -um	**erō**	*I shall have been praised*
laudābāris	*you were...*	laudātus, -a, -um **es**	*you have been...*	laudātus, -a, -um	**eris**	*you will have been...*
laudābātur	*he was...*	laudātus, -a, -um **est**	*he has been...*	laudātus, -a, -um	**erit**	*he will have been...*
laudābāmur	*we were...*	laudātī, -ae, -a **sumus**	*we have been...*	laudātī, -ae, -a	**erimus**	*we shall have been...*
laudābāminī	*you were...*	laudātī, -ae, -a **estis**	*you have been...*	laudātī, -ae, -a	**eritis**	*you will have been...*
laudābantur	*they were...*	laudātī, -ae, -a **sunt**	*they have been...*	laudātī, -ae, -a	**erunt**	*they will have been...*

Second Conjugation

PRINCIPAL PARTS OF MONEŌ

				SUPINE
moneō	*I warn*	**monuī**	*I have warned*	monitum
monēre	*to warn*	**monitus**	*warned*	monitū

PARTICIPLES
Present Act.: monēns   *warning*
Perfect Pass.: monitus, -a, -um
Future Act.: monitūrus, -a, -um
Gerundive: monendus, -a, -um

GERUND
Nom.: monēre
Gen.: monendī
Dat.: monendō
Acc.: monendum
Abl.: monendō

INFINITIVES
ACTIVE
Present: **monēre**
Perfect: **monuisse**
Future: **monitūrus esse**
PASSIVE
Present: mōnērī
Perfect: monitus esse
Future: monitum īrī

INDICATIVE ACTIVE

Present	Perfect
moneō	monuī
monēs	monuistī
monet	monuit
monēmus	monuimus
monētis	monuistis
monent	monuērunt
Imperfect	*Pluperfect*
monēbam	monueram
monēbās	monuerās
monēbat	monuerat
monēbāmus	monuerāmus
monēbātis	monuerātis
monēbant	monuerant
Future	*Future Perfect*
monēbō	monuerō
monēbis	monueris
monēbit	monuerit
monēbimus	monuerimus
monēbitis	monueritis
monēbunt	monuerint

INDICATIVE PASSIVE

Present	Perfect	
moneor	monitus, -a, -um	**sum**
monēris	monitus, -a, -um	**es**
monētur	monitus, -a, -um	**est**
monēmur	monitī, -ae, -a	**sumus**
monēminī	monitī, -ae, -a	**estis**
monentur	monitī, -ae, -a	**sunt**
Imperfect	*Pluperfect*	
monēbar	monitus, -a, -um	**eram**
monēbāris	monitus, -a, -um	**erās**
monēbātur	monitus, -a, -um	**erat**
monēbāmur	monitī, -ae, -a	**erāmus**
monēbāminī	monitī, -ae, -a	**erātis**
monēbantur	monitī, -ae, -a	**erant**
Future	*Future Perfect*	
monēbor	monitus, -a, -um	**erō**
monēberis	monitus, -a, -um	**eris**
monēbitur	monitus, -a, -um	**erit**
monēbimur	monitī, -ae, -a	**erimus**
monēbiminī	monitī, -ae, -a	**eritis**
monēbuntur	monitī, -ae, -a	**erunt**

IMPERATIVE ACT.
PRESENT
Sing.: monē
Plur.: monēte

IMPERATIVE PASS.
PRESENT
Sing.: monēre
Plur.: monēminī

SUBJUNCTIVE ACT.

Present	Perfect
moneam	monuerim
moneās	monuerīs
moneat	monuerit
moneāmus	monuerīmus
moneātis	monuerītis
moneant	monuerint
Imperfect	*Pluperfect*
monērem	monuissem
monērēs	monuissēs
monēret	monuisset
monērēmus	monuissēmus
monērētis	monuissetis
monērent	monuissent

SUBJUNCTIVE PASS.

Present	Perfect	
monear	monitus, -a, -um	**sim**
moneāris	monitus, -a, -um	**sīs**
moneātur	monitus, -a, -um	**sit**
moneāmur	monitī, -ae, -a	**sīmus**
moneāminī	monitī, -ae, -a	**sītis**
moneantur	monitī, -ae, -a	**sint**
Imperfect	*Pluperfect*	
monērer	monitus, -a, -um	**essem**
monērēris	monitus, -a, -um	**essēs**
monērētur	monitus, -a, -um	**esset**
monērēmur	monitī, -ae, -a	**essēmus**
monērēminī	monitī, -ae, -a	**essētis**
monērentur	monitī, -ae, -a	**essent**

* *Graphic Latin Grammar* was prepared by James P. Humphreys and is also available on laminated, hole-punched cards from Bolchazy-Carducci Publishers, Inc. www.bolchazy.com

Third Conjugation

PRINCIPAL PARTS OF DŪCŌ

dūcō	*I lead*	**dūxī**	*I have led*
dūcere	*to lead*	**ductus**	*having been led*

The future active of the third conjugation is formed by adding -am, -ēs, -et, etc. to the present stem minus **-e**. To form the passive, -ar, -ēris, ētur, etc. are added to the present stem minus **-e**.

INDICATIVE ACTIVE

Present	Perfect
dūcō	dūxī
dūcis	dūxistī
dūcit	dūxit
dūcimus	dūximus
dūcitis	dūxistis
dūcunt	dūxērunt
Imperfect	*Pluperfect*
dūcēbam	dūxeram
dūcēbās	dūxerās
dūcēbat	dūxerat
dūcēbāmus	dūxerāmus
dūcēbātis	dūxerātis
dūcēbant	dūxerant
Future	*Future Perf.*
dūcam	dūxerō
dūcēs	dūxeris
dūcet	dūxerit
dūcēmus	dūxerimus
dūcētis	dūxeritis
dūcent	dūxerint

INDICATIVE PASSIVE

Present	Perfect	
dūcor	ductus, -a, -um	**sum**
dūceris	ductus, -a, -um	**es**
dūcitur	ductus, -a, -um	**est**
dūcimur	ductī, -ae, -a	**sumus**
dūciminī	ductī, -ae, -a	**estis**
dūcuntur	ductī, -ae, -a	**sunt**
Imperfect	*Pluperfect*	
dūcēbar	ductus, -a, -um	**eram**
dūcēbāris	ductus, -a, -um	**erās**
dūcēbātur	ductus, -a, -um	**erat**
dūcēbāmur	ductī, -ae, -a	**erāmus**
dūcēbāminī	ductī, -ae, -a	**erātis**
dūcēbantur	ductī, -ae, -a	**erant**
Future	*Future Perfect*	
dūcar	ductus, -a, -um	**erō**
dūcēris	ductus, -a, -um	**eris**
dūcētur	ductus, -a, -um	**erit**
dūcēmur	ductī, -ae, -a	**erimus**
dūcēminī	ductī, -ae, -a	**eritis**
dūcentur	ductī, -ae, -a	**erunt**

SUBJUNCTIVE ACT.

Present	Perfect
dūcam	dūxerim
dūcās	dūxerīs
dūcat	dūxerit
dūcāmus	dūxerīmus
dūcātis	dūxerītis
dūcant	dūxerint
Imperfect	*Pluperfect*
dūcerem	dūxissem
dūcerēs	dūxissēs
dūceret	dūxisset
dūcerēmus	dūxissēmus
dūcerētis	dūxissētis
dūcerent	dūxissent

IMPERATIVE ACTIVE

Sing.: dūc[1]
Plur.: dūcite

[1]There are 4 verbs whose imperative omits the final "e" in the singular: dīc, dūc, fer, fac.

SUBJUNCTIVE PASSIVE

Present	Perfect	
dūcar	ductus, -a, -um	**sim**
dūcāris	ductus, -a, -um	**sīs**
dūcātur	ductus, -a, -um	**sit**
dūcāmur	ductī, -ae, -a	**sīmus**
dūcāminī	ductī, -ae, -a	**sītis**
dūcantur	ductī, -ae, -a	**sint**
Imperfect	*Pluperfect*	
dūcerer	ductus, -a, -um	**essem**
dūcerēris	ductus, -a, -um	**essēs**
dūcerētur	ductus, -a, -um	**esset**
dūcerēmur	ductī, -ae, -a	**essēmus**
dūcerēminī	ductī, -ae, -a	**essētis**
dūcerentur	ductī, -ae, -a	**essent**

IMPERATIVE PASSIVE

Sing.: dūcere
Plur.: dūciminī

PARTICIPLES

Present Active: dūcēns, dūcentis
Perf. Passive: ductus, -a, -um
Fut. Active: ductūrus, -a, -um
Gerundive: dūcendus, -a, -um

INFINITIVES

Active
Pres.: dūcere
Perf.: dūxisse
Fut.: ductūrus esse
Passive
Pres.: dūcī[2]
Perf.: ductus esse
Fut.: ductum īrī

[2]To form the present passive infinitive, replace the -ere of the active form with -ī.

SUPINE

ductum
ductū

GERUND

Nom.: dūcere
Gen.: dūcendī
Dat.: dūcendō
Acc.: dūcendum
Abl.: dūcendō

Fourth Conjugation

PRINCIPAL PARTS OF AUDIŌ

audiō	*I hear*	**audīvī**	*I have heard*
audīre	*to hear*	**audītus**	*having been heard*

INDICATIVE ACTIVE

Present	Perfect
audiō	audīvī
audīs	audīvistī
audit	audīvit
audīmus	audīvimus
audītis	audīvistis
audiunt	audīvērunt
Imperfect	*Pluperfect*
audiēbam	audīveram
audiēbās	audīverās
audiēbat	audīverat
audiēbāmus	audīverāmus
audiēbātis	audīverātis
audiēbant	audīverant
Future	*Future Perf.*
audiam	audīverō
audiēs	audīveris
audiet	audīverit
audiēmus	audīverimus
audiētis	audīveritis
audient	audīverint

INDICATIVE PASSIVE

Present	Perfect	
audior	audītus, -a, -um	**sum**
audīris	audītus, -a, -um	**es**
audītur	audītus, -a, -um	**est**
audīmur	audītī, -ae, -a	**sumus**
audīminī	audītī, -ae, -a	**estis**
audiuntur	audītī, -ae, -a	**sunt**
Imperfect	*Pluperfect*	
audiēbar	audītus, -a, -um	**eram**
audiēbāris	audītus, -a, -um	**erās**
audiēbātur	audītus, -a, -um	**erat**
audiēbāmur	audītī, -ae, -a	**erāmus**
audiēbāminī	audītī, -ae, -a	**erātis**
audiēbantur	audītī, -ae, -a	**erant**
Future	*Future Perfect*	
audiar	audītus, -a, -um	**erō**
audiēris	audītus, -a, -um	**eris**
audiētur	audītus, -a, -um	**erit**
audiēmur	audītī, -ae, -a	**erimus**
audiēminī	audītī, -ae, -a	**eritis**
audientur	audītī, -ae, -a	**erunt**

SUBJUNCTIVE ACT.

Present	Perfect
audiam	audīverim
audiās	audīverīs
audiat	audīverit
audiāmus	audīverīmus
audiātis	audīverītis
audiant	audīverint
Imperfect	*Pluperfect*
audīrem	audīvissem
audīrēs	audīvissēs
audīret	audīvisset
audīrēmus	audīvissēmus
audīrētis	audīvissētis
audīrent	audīvissent

IMPERATIVE ACT.

Sing.: audī
Plur.: audīte

IMPERATIVE PASS.

Sing.: audīre
Plur.: audīminī

SUBJUNCTIVE PASSIVE

Present	Perfect	
audiar	audītus, -a, -um	**sim**
audiāris	audītus, -a, -um	**sīs**
audiātur	audītus, -a, -um	**sit**
audiāmur	audītī, -ae, -a	**sīmus**
audiāminī	audītī, -ae, -a	**sītis**
audiantur	audītī, -ae, -a	**sint**
Imperfect	*Pluperfect*	
audīrer	audītus, -a, -um	**essem**
audīrēris	audītus, -a, -um	**essēs**
audīrētur	audītus, -a, -um	**esset**
audīrēmur	audītī, -ae, -a	**essēmus**
audīrēminī	audītī, -ae, -a	**essētis**
audīrentur	audītī, -ae, -a	**essent**

PARTICIPLES

Present Active: audiēns
Perf. Passive: audītus, -a, -um
Fut. Active: audītūrus, -a, -um
Gerundive: audiendus, -a, -um

SUPINE

audītum, audītū

INFINITIVES[1]

Active
Pres.: audīre
Perf.: audīvisse
Fut.: audītūrus esse
Passive
Pres.: audīrī
Perf.: audītus esse
Fut.: audītum īrī

[1]The present passive infinitive of the 1st, 2nd, and 4th conjugations is formed by replacing the final -e of the present active infin. with an ī.

GERUND

Nom.: audīre
Gen.: audiendī
Dat.: audiendō
Acc.: audiendum
Abl.: audiendō

2. ORTHOGRAPHIC-CHANGING AND IRREGULAR VERBS

The -io Verbs of the 3rd Conjugation

PRINCIPAL PARTS OF CAPIŌ

capiō	*I seize*	**cēpī**	*I have seized*
capere	*to seize*	**captus**	*having been seized*

INDICATIVE

The six tenses of the indicative active are conjugated like audiō (4th conjugation) except that the -i of capiō is short throughout the present tense.
In the indicative passive, the second person singular, present passive, differs from its parallel in audiō: caperis, audīris.

SUBJUNCTIVE

The imperfect subjunctive of capiō, both active and passive, is formed from the 2nd principal part, capere, while audiō performs the same way. For example:

ACTIVE		PASSIVE	
caperem	audīrem	caperer	audīrer
etc.	etc.	etc.	etc.

INFINITIVES

Active	**Passive**
Pres.: capere	*Pres.*: capī
Perf.: cēpisse	*Perf.*: captus esse
Fut.: captūrus esse	*Fut.*: captum īrī

IMPERATIVE

Active	**Passive**
cape	capere
capite	capiminī

GERUND AND SUPINE

These are formed like counterparts in audiō.

The Irregular Verb Sum

PRINCIPAL PARTS

sum	*I am*	**fuī**	*I have been*
esse	*to be*	**futūrus**	*being about to be*

INDICATIVE

Present	Perfect
sum	fuī
es	fuistī
est	fuit
sumus	fuimus
estis	fuistis
sunt	fuērunt
Imperf.	*Pluperf.*
eram	fueram
erās	fuerās
erat	fuerat
erāmus	fuerāmus
erātis	fuerātis
erant	fuerant
Future	*Fut. Perf.*
erō	fuerō
eris	fueris
erit	fuerit
erimus	fuerimus
eritis	fueritis
erunt	fuerint

SUBJUNCTIVE

Present	Perfect
sim	fuerim
sīs	fueris
sit	fuerit
sīmus	fuerīmus
sītis	fuerītis
sint	fuerint
Imperf.	*Pluperf.*
essem	fuissem
essēs	fuissēs
esset	fuisset
essēmus	fuissēmus
essētis	fuissētis
essent	fuissent

IMPERATIVE[1]

Present
es — *be thou*
este — *be ye*

[1]The future imperative of sum, esto, sometimes means *So be it.*

INFINITIVES

Present	Perfect
esse	fuisse
Future	
futūrus esse	

PARTICIPLE

Future
futūrus, -a, -um

The Irregular Verb Possum

PRINCIPAL PARTS

possum	*I am able*	**potuī**	*I have been able*
posse	*to be able*		

INDICATIVE

Present	Perfect
possum	potuī
potes	potuistī
potest	potuit
possumus	potuimus
potestis	potuistis
possunt	potuērunt
Imperfect	*Pluperf.*
poteram	potueram
poterās	potuerās
poterat	potuerat
poterāmus	potuerāmus
poterātis	potuerātis
poterant	potuerant
Future	*Fut. Perf.*
poterō	potuerō
poteris	potueris
poterit	potuerit
poterimus	potuerimus
poteritis	potueritis
poterunt	potuerint

SUBJUNCTIVE

Present	Perfect
possim	potuerim
possīs	potueris
possit	potuerit
possīmus	potuerīmus
possītis	potuerītis
possint	potuerint
Imperfect	*Pluperf.*
possem	potuissem
possēs	potuissēs
posset	potuisset
possēmus	potuissēmus
possētis	potuissētis
possent	potuissent

INFINITIVES

Present
posse
Perfect
potuisse

PARTICIPLE

Present
potēns (*Gen.* potentis)

Deponent Verbs (Passive in form; active in meaning)

There are deponent verbs in all four conjugations. All are regularly passive in form. Exceptions are the future infinitive and the present and future participles, which are active in form (see cōnor, on the right).

cōnāns	*trying* (1st conjug.)
cōnātus	*having tried*
cōnātūrus	*being about to try*
cōnandus	*worthy to be tried*

Present: cōnārī *to try*
Perfect: cōnātus esse *to have tried*
Future: cōnātūrus esse *to be about to try*

The Irregular Verb Ferō

PRINCIPAL PARTS

ferō	*I bear*	tulī	*I have borne*
ferre	*to bear*	lātus	*having been borne*

INDICATIVE ACTIVE

Present	Perfect
ferō	tulī
fers	tulistī
fert	tulit
ferimus	tulimus
fertis	tulistis
ferunt	tulērunt
Imperf.	*Pluperf.*
ferēbam	tuleram
ferēbās	tulerās
ferēbat	tulerat
etc.	*etc.*
Future	*Fut. Perf.*
feram	tulerō
ferēs	tuleris
feret	tulerit
etc.	*etc.*

INDICATIVE PASSIVE

Present	Perfect
feror	lātus, -a, -um **sum**
ferris	lātus, -a, -um **es**
fertur	lātus, -a, -um **est**
ferimur	*etc.*
feriminī	
feruntur	
Imperf.	*Pluperfect*
ferēbar	lātus, -a, -um **eram**
ferēbāris	lātus, -a, -um **erās**
ferēbātur	lātus, -a, -um **erat**
etc.	*etc.*
Future	*Future Perfect*
ferar	lātus, -a, -um **erō**
ferēris	lātus, -a, -um **eris**
ferētur	lātus, -a, -um **erit**
etc.	*etc.*

SUBJUNCTIVE ACTIVE

Present	Perfect
feram	tulerim
ferās	tuleris
ferat	tulerit
etc.	*etc.*
Imperf.	*Pluperf.*
ferrem	tulissem
ferrēs	tulissēs
ferret	tulisset
etc.	*etc.*

SUBJUNCTIVE PASSIVE

Present	Perfect
ferar	lātus, -a, -um **sim**
ferāris	lātus, -a, -um **sīs**
ferātur	lātus, -a, -um **sit**
etc.	*etc.*
Imperf.	*Pluperfect*
ferrer	lātus, -a, -um **essem**
ferrēris	lātus, -a, -um **essēs**
ferrētur	lātus, -a, -um **esset**
etc.	*etc.*

IMPERATIVE ACTIVE

Present
Sing.: fer
Plur.: ferte

INFINITIVES—ACTIVE

Present
ferre
Perfect
tulisse
Future
lātūrus esse

PARTICIPLES—ACTIVE

Present
ferēns
Future
lātūrus, -a, -um

IMPERATIVE—PASSIVE

Present
Sing.: ferre
Plur.: feriminī

INFINITIVES—PASSIVE

Present
ferrī
Perfect
lātus esse
Future
lātum īrī

PARTICIPLES—PASSIVE

Perfect
lātus, -a, -um
Gerundive
ferendus, -a, -um

SUPINE	GERUND	
lātum	*Nom.:* ferre	*Acc.:* ferend**um**
lātū	*Gen.:* ferendī	*Abl.:* ferendō
	Dat.: ferendō	

The Irregular Verbs Volō, Nōlō, and Mālō
Nōlō is made up from nē-volō, while mālō is curtailed from magis-volō.

PRINCIPAL PARTS

volō	*I wish*
velle	*to wish*
voluī	*I have wished*

Note: With the exception of the present tense, the forms of nōlō and mālō are similar to volō. For forms not given below, see volō, which is complete.

INDICATIVE

Present	Perfect
volō	voluī
vīs	voluistī
vult	voluit
volumus	voluimus
vultis	voluistis
volunt	voluērunt
Imperfect	*Pluperfect*
volēbam	volueram
volēbās	voluerās
volēbat	voluerat
volēbāmus	voluerāmus
volēbātis	voluerātis
volēbant	voluerant
Future	*Future Perf.*
volam	voluerō
volēs	volueris
volet	voluerit
volēmus	voluerimus
volētis	volueritis
volent	voluerint

SUBJUNCTIVE

Present	Perfect
velim	voluerim
velīs	voluerīs
velit	voluerit
velīmus	voluerīmus
velītis	voluerītis
velint	voluerint
Imperfect	*Pluperfect*
vellem	voluissem
vellēs	voluissēs
vellet	voluisset
vellēmus	voluissēmus
vellētis	voluissētis
vellent	voluissent

PRINCIPAL PARTS

mālō	*I prefer*
mālle	*to prefer*
māluī	*I have prefered*

INDIC.	SUBJ.
Present	*Present*
mālō	mālim
māvīs	mālīs
māvult	mālit
mālumus	mālīmus
māvultis	mālītis
mālunt	mālint

INFINITIVES
mālle
māluisse

IMPERATIVE
(none)

INFINITIVES
Present: velle
Perfect: voluisse

PARTICIPLES
Present: volēns
(Gen. volentis*)*

PRINCIPAL PARTS

nōlō	*I do not wish*
nōlle	*to be unwilling*
nōluī	*I have been unwilling*

INDICATIVE	SUBJUNCTIVE
Present	*Present*
nōlō	nōlim
nōn vīs	nōlīs
nōn vult	nōlit
nōlumus	nōlīmus
nōn vultis	nōlītis
nōlunt	nōlint

IMPERATIVE[1]
Sing.: nōlī
Plur.: nōlīte

(These forms, plus a complementary infinitive, express a negative command.)

[1] Mālō and volō do not have imperative forms. Mālō is deficient in participles also.

INFINITIVES
nōlle
nōluisse

PARTICIPLES
nōlēns
nōlentis *(Gen.)*

The Irregular Verb Fiō

PRINCIPAL PARTS

fīō	*I am made*
fierī	*to be made*
factus	*having been made*

Note: Fīō is the irregular passive of faciō. Even though it is conjugated actively in the present, future, imperfect, it always has passive meaning.

INDICATIVE

Present	Perfect 1
fīō	factus, -a, -um **sum**
fīs	*etc.*
fit	
fīmus	
fītis	
fīunt	
Imperf.	*Pluperfect*
fīēbam	factus, -a, -um **eram**
fīēbās	*etc.*
fīēbat	
fīēbāmus	
fīēbātis	
fīēbant	
Future	*Future Perfect*
fīam	factus, -a, -um **erō**
fīēs	*etc.*
fīet	
fīēmus	
fīētis	
fīent	

SUBJUNCTIVE

Present	Perfect
fīam	factus, -a,
fīās	-um **sim**
fīat	*etc.*
fīāmus	
fīātis	
fīant	
Imperf.	*Pluperfect*
fierem	factus, -a,
fierēs	-um **essem**
fieret	*etc.*
fierēmus	
fierētis	
fierent	

[1] Most compounds of faciō become -ficiō, while factus becomes -fectus. They are conjugated ike capiō. But the passive of satisfaciō is satisfiō.

PARTICIPLES
Present: (none)
Perfect: factus
Gerundive: faciendus

INFINITIVES
Present: fierī
Perfect: factus esse
Future: factum īrī

The Irregular Verb eō[1]

PRINCIPAL PARTS
INDICATIVE

eō	*I go*	iī (īvī) *I have gone*
īre	*to go*	itum (est) *it has been gone*

Present	Future	Pluperf.
eō	ībō	ieram
īs	ībis	ierās
it	ībit	ierat
īmus	ībimus	ierāmus
ītis	ībitis	ierātis
eunt	ībunt	ierant
Imperf.	*Perfect*	*Fut. Perf.*
ībam	iī	ierō
ībās	iistī	ieris
ībat	iit	ierit
ībāmus	iimus	ierimus
ībātis	iistis	ieritis
ībant	iērunt	ierint

PARTICIPLES
Present: iēns (euntis)
Future: itūrus, -a, -um
Gerundive: eundus

SUBJUNCTIVE

Present	Perfect
eam	ierim
eās	ierīs
eat	ierit
eāmus	ierīmus
eātis	ierītis
eant	ierint
Imperf.	*Pluperfect*
īrem	iissem (īssem)
īrēs	iissēs
īret	iisset
īrēmus	iissēmus
īrētis	iissētis
īrent	iissent

IMPERATIVE
Present
Sing.: ī
Plur.: īte

INFINITIVES
Pres.: īre
Perf.: iisse
Fut.: itūrus esse

GERUND
Nom.: īre
Gen.: eundī
Dat.: eundō
Acc.: eund**um**
Abl.: eundō

SUPINE
itum *to go*
itū *to go*

[1] Adeō, ineō, and trānseō are transitive and may therefore be conjugated in the passive. Queō and nequeō are conjugated like eō.

The Defective Verbs Coepī, Ōdī, and Meminī

These verbs have forms in the perfect system only, the present, imperfect, and future tenses having been displaced. Coepī is the only one of the three to have passive forms; the other two are conjugated only in the per fect active systems. The conjugations of all three are otherwise perfectly regular and have not been reproduced below.

PRINCIPAL PARTS

coepī	*I began* [1]
coepisse	*to have begun*
coeptus	*begun*

(Note *past* meaning.)

ōdī	*I hate*
ōdisse	*to hate*
ōsus	*hated, hating*

(Note *present* meaning.)

meminī	*I remember*
meminisse	*to remember*

(Note *present* meaning.)

INFINITIVES
Perfect
coepisse
Future
coeptūrus esse

Perfect: ōdisse
Future: ōsūrus esse

Perfect: meminisse

PARTICIPLES
Perfect
coeptus
Future
coeptūrus

Perfect: ōsus
Future: ōsūrus

Ōdī lacks imperatives.

IMPERATIVE
Sing.: mementō
Plur.: mementōte

[1] For a present meaning of *"begin,"* use incipiō. Coepī has no imperative forms.

Indicative Mood

1. The historical present is used to make the past more vivid: Mīlitēs iter **faciunt**. *The soldiers made a journey.*
2. **Iam** with any expression of time, plus the present, equals the English perfect: **Iam** diū in Americā **est**. *He has been*. **Iam** plus the imperfect equals the English pluperfect: Iam multōs annōs **rēgnābat**. *He had been...*
3. **Dum** *(while)* plus the present equals the English past. **Dum pugnant**, imperātor pervēnit. *While they were fighting...*
4. **Quamquam** and **etsī** *(although)* take any tense of the indicative: **Quamquam** Rōmae est... *Although he is in Rome...*
5. **Postquam** *(after)*, **ubi** *(when)*, **simul atque** *(as soon as)*, plus the Latin perfect, equal English pluperfect: **Postquam** ad oppidum **pervēnit**... *After he had arrived at the town...*
6. Causal clauses introduced by **quod** or **quoniam** employ the indicative: Fortissimī sunt illī virī **quod** longissimē **absunt**. *Those men are the bravest because they are the farthest away.*
7. Temporal clauses introduced by **cum** and showing true time are in the indicative: Tum **cum** multī rēs magnās **āmīserant**... *At the time when many men had lost great fortunes...*
8. Relative clauses are usually in the indicative: ...in partēs trēs, quārum ūnam **incolunt** Belgae ...*into three parts, of which the Belgians inhabit one.* (For relative clauses in subjunctive, see below.)

Subjunctive Mood—Independent Uses

1. Deliberative or dubitative questions (rhetorical or expressing doubt) use the subjunctive: Quid **agam**, iūdicēs? *What am I to do, jurors?*
2. Statements of potential (possible action) employ subjunctive: **Dīcat** quispiam... *Someone may say...*
3. Commands of the 1st or 3rd person are in subjunctive (hortatory subjunctive): **Laudēmus**... *Let us praise...* **Laudet**... *Let him praise...* (BUT 2nd person commands are in imperative: **Laudā**... *(You) Praise...*)
4. Wishes possible of fulfillment are in present subjunctive: Utinam **vīvat**! *Oh that he might live (go on living)!* Wishes impossible of fulfillment are in imperfect or pluperfect subjunctive: Utinam **vīveret**! *If he were only alive!*
5. Conditional ("if-then") sentences possible of fulfillment employ present subjunctive in both clauses: Sī pater tēcum **loquātur**, nōnne audīre **debeās**? *If your father speaks, shouldn't you listen?*
6. Conditional sentences impossible of fulfillment (or contrary to fact) employ the imperfect subjunctive or the pluperfect subjunctive: Sī hoc **accidisset**, Clōdius nōn mortuus **esset**. *If this had happened, Clōdius would not have died.*

Some Special Verb Rules

1. A finite verb agrees with its subject in person and number.
2. A question expecting the answer "maybe" has the suffix **-ne** attached to the most important word in the sentence. A question introduced by **nōnne** expects "yes;" **num** expects "no."
3. Verbs meaning *favor, help, please, trust* (and their opposites) and *believe, persuade, command, obey, serve, resist, envy, pardon,* and *spare* take the dative case.
4. Many Verbs compounded with **ad, ante, con, in, inter, ob, post, prae, prō, sub,** and **super** take the dative case.
5. The direct object of a transitive verb is in the accusative case.
6. The subject of an infinitive is in the accusative case.
7. The deponent verbs, **ūtor, fruor, fungor, potior, vēscor** take the ablative case.
8. Verbs of fearing take the subjunctive with **nē** *(that)* and **ut** or **nē nōn** *(that not)*.
9. Attraction means that a verb ordinarily indicative is attracted into the subjunctive mood by the proximity of another subjunctive.

Subjunctive Mood—Dependent Uses

1. Any subordinate clause introduced by an interrogative word is an indirect question. It ordinarily depends upon a verb of *knowing, telling, seeing, hearing,* or any expression of uncertainty. The verb of the indirect question goes in the subjunctive. The tense of the subjunctive clause depends upon whether the action of the indicative verb in the main clause is continuing or complete. There are two sequences of tenses (depending upon the two possible times of the main verb):
   A. Primary (main verb in present time):
   Scit quid **faciam**. *He knows what I am doing.*
   Scit quid **factūrus sim**.[1] *He knows what I shall do.*
   Scit quid **fēcerim**. *He knows what I did.*
   B. Secondary (main verb in past time):
   Scīvit quid **facerem**. *He knew what I was doing.*
   Scīvit quid **factūrus essem**.[1] *He knew what I was going to do.*
   Scīvit quid **fēcissem**. *He knew what I had done.*

   [1]Since in this instance a future form of the subjunctive is needed, the present and imperfect forms of the verb **sum** are used, along with the future participle, to take the place of the missing form.

2. Purpose Clauses — Adverbial. The purpose clause modifies the introducing verb. Venit ut mē **videat**. *He comes to (literally, in order that he may) see me.*
3. Purpose Clauses — Relative. The purpose clause is adjectival. Mīsit explōrātōrem quī mīlitēs **dūceret**. *He sent a scout to lead the soldiers.*
4. Purpose Clauses — Substantive. The clause is the object of a verb of asking, commanding, etc. Eīs persuādēbit ut **exeant**. *He will persuade them to leave.*
5. Result Clauses — Adverbial. Tam fortis erat ut vincī nōn **posset**. *He was so brave that he could not be conquered.*
6. Result Clauses — Substantive. Accidit ut **sit** lūna plēna. *It happens that the moon is full.*
7. After verbs of fearing. Germānī verēbantur nē Caesar cōpiās trāns Rhēnum **trādūceret**. *The Germans feared that Caesar would lead troops across the Rhine. Note:* After verbs of fearing, **nē** replaces **ut,** and **ut** becomes negative "that not."
8. In **Cum** Clauses (when **cum** means *when, since,* or *although*). Cum id **nūntiātum esset**... *When this was announced...* Quae cum ita **sint**... *Since this is so...* Cum prīmī ōrdinēs **concidissent**... *Although the first ranks had fallen...*
9. After **Dum** (meaning *until*). Dum relīquae nāvēs **convenīrent**, ad nōnam hōram exspectāvit. *He waited until (to) the ninth hour, until the rest of the ships would assemble.*
10. Clauses of comparison introduced by **utsi, velutsi, quasi.** Dīcit velutsi **sit** āmēns. *He speaks as if he were mad.*
11. Negative expressions of doubt and hindering: Nōn est dubium quīn mīlitēs **sint** fortēs. *There is no doubt that the soldiers are brave.*
12. Relative Clause of Description — Erat mīles quī fortiter **pugnāret**. *He was a soldier who would fight bravely.*

Syntax of the Infinitive

1. In indirect statement when the statement made by a speaker is reported by someone, the subject is in the accusative case, the verb becomes an infinitive, and any subordinate verb becomes subjunctive. In deciding upon the tense of any subordinate verb, the sequence of tenses is followed. In deciding upon the tense of the infinitive, the problem may be resolved by returning the sentence to direct statement, and then using the same tense of the infinitive.
   Dīcit sē **venīre**. *He says that he is coming.* (direct: *I am coming.*)
   Dīxit sē **venīre**. *He said that he was coming.* (direct: *I am coming.*)
   Dīcit sē **vēnisse**. *He says that he has come.* (direct: *I have come.*)
   Dīxit sē **vēnisse**. *He said that he had come.* (direct: *I have come.*)
   Dīcit sē **ventūrum esse**. *He says that he will come.* (direct: *I shall come.*)
   Dīxit sē **ventūrum esse**. *He said that he would come.* (direct: *I shall come.*)
   Subordinate clauses occurring within an indirect statement are often conditions. In such cases, the "if clause" is in the subjunctive and the "conclusion" is an infinitive construction. Dīxit sī īret, nēminem secūtūrum **esse**. *He said that if he should go, no one should follow.*
2. Complementary Infinitive. An infinitive without a subject is used to complete the action of certain verbs:

possum — *I am able*	statuō — *I determine*
volō — *I wish*	cōnor — *I try*
nōlō — *I do not wish*	temptō — *I try*
mālō — *I prefer*	audeō — *I dare*
cupiō — *I desire*	dēbeō — *I ought*
patior — *I allow*	constituō — *I decide*
dubitō — *I hesitate*	parō — *I prepare*
incipiō — *I begin*	dēsistō — *I cease*
	videor — *I seem*

   Bellum **īnferre** possunt... *They are able to make war on...*
3. Objective Infinitive. Many verbs which ordinarily would take a complementary infinitive take an objective infinitive when the subject of the verb is different from the subject of the infinitive. Eum **abīre** iussērunt. *They ordered him to go away.*
4. Subjective Infinitive. Facile est hoc **facere**. *To do this is easy.*
5. Historical Infinitive. The infinitive, with a nominative subject, is sometimes used to express past time more vividly. Ego **īnstāre** ut mihi respondēret. *I kept urging him to reply to me.*

Syntax of Participles

1. Participles are verbals which perform as adjectives. Mīlitēs **moritūrī** proelium commīsērunt. *The soldiers who were about to die engaged in battle.*
2. Future passive participles (sometimes called gerundives) express necessity or obligation. Vir **laudandus**. *A man worthy to be praised.* The future passive participle used with some form of sum is called the second periphrastic conjugation. Puella **est amanda**. *The girl ought to be loved.*
3. The future active participle combined with sum (first periphrastic conjugation) is a way of expressing futurity, even in past time. Ducem **monitūrus eram**. *I was about to advise the general.*
4. The gerund is a verbal noun which is declinable only in the singular. The gerund, as a verb, may take an object. Ars bene **disserendī**... *The art of speaking well...*
5. The supine, ending in **-um,** is used to express purpose with verbs of motion. **Pugnātum** vēnērunt. *They came to fight.* Ending in **-ū,** the supine is used with certain adjectives. Difficile **factū**... *Difficult to do...*

Nouns are the names of persons, places, or things. In Latin, nouns, pronouns, and adjectives are inflected to show their grammatical relations to the other words in the sentence. These inflectional endings are usually equivalent to prepositional phrases in English.

The names of the cases and their functions are as follows:

LATIN CASE	USE IN THE SENTENCE	ENGLISH CASE	EXAMPLE
Nominative	Subject or subj. complement.	Nominative.	Puer (the or a boy)
Genitive	Shows possession and other relationships.	Possessive or the objective, with "of."	Puerī (of the boy, or of a boy)
Dative	Indirect object and other relationships.	Objective, often with "to" or "for."	Puerō (to or for the boy)
Accusative	Direct object.	Objective.	Puerum (boy, or the boy)
Ablative	Occurs in adverbial phrases, usually with a preposition.	Objective, as object of many prepositions.	Puerō (by the boy, from, with, on, at, etc.)

There are two additional cases which occur infrequently, and are not usually given with the declensions:

Vocative	Case of address. (The Latin inflectional ending is the same as in the nominative with exceptions noted, p. 7.)	Nominative of address.	Puer! (Boy!)
Locative	Case of "place at which," with cities, towns, small islands, and **domus** (home) only.	Objective, with "at."	Rōmae (at Rome)

Inflection in General

The inflectional ending of a word shows its *number, gender,* and *case.* The general concepts of number and case are similar to their counterparts in English (singular-plural, case structure outlined above). However, *gender* in Latin is often *grammatical* only, and unrelated to *natural* gender. Although there are the same three genders (masculine, feminine, neuter) in Latin as in English, it is not uncommon for a word like nauta (sailor), which is naturally male, to appear in a feminine declension (1st declension). Inflected words are comprised of two parts: the *base* and the inflected portion. The *base* is that part of the word which remains unchanged, and the base of any noun may be determined by removing the ending of the *genitive singular* form. The base of **terra** is **terr-**; the base of **ager** is **agr-**, and so on.

4. NOUNS
First and Second Declension Nouns

The gender of most 1st declension nouns is feminine. That of most 2nd declension nouns is neuter (ending in **-um**) or masculine (ending in **-us** or **-er**).

	1st Declension — Fem.		2nd Declension — Masc.		2nd Declension — Neut.				2nd Declension Masc. Ending in -er			
	Sing.	Plur.	Sing.	Plur.	Sing.	Plur.	Sing.	Plur.	Sing.	Plur.	Sing.	Plur.
Nom.	terra (land)	-ae	dominus (lord)	-ī	caelum (sky)	-a	ager (field)	agrī	puer (boy)	-ī		
Gen.	terrae	-ārum	dominī	-ōrum	caelī	-ōrum	agrī	-ōrum	puerī	-ōrum		
Dat.	terrae	-īs	dominō	-īs	caelō	-īs	agrō	-īs	puerō	-īs		
Acc.	terram	-ās	dominum	-ōs	caelum	-a	agrum	-ōs	puerum	-ōs		
Abl.	terrā	-īs	dominō	-īs	caelō	-īs	agrō	-īs	puerō	-īs		

Third Declension Nouns

The trademark of the 3rd declension is the ending **-is** in the genitive singular. It is added to the base. All genders are represented in the 3rd declension.[1]

	(light)		(soldier)		(ship)		(night)		(sea)		(type)		(river)	
	Sing.	Plur.	Sing.	Plur.	Sing.	Plur.	Sing.	Plur.	Sing.	Plur.	Sing.	Plur.	Sing.	Plur.
Nom.	lūx	lūcēs	mīles	mīlitēs	nāvis	-ēs	nox	noctēs	mare	-ia	genus	genera	flūmen	flūmina
Gen.	lūcis	-um	mīlitis	-um	nāvis	-ium	noctis	-ium	maris	-ium	generis	-um	flūminis	-um
Dat.	lūcī	-ibus	mīlitī	-ibus	nāvī	-ibus	noctī	-ibus	marī	-ibus	generī	-ibus	flūminī	-ibus
Acc.	lūcem	-ēs	mīlitem	-ēs	nāvem	-ēs (-īs)	noctem	-ēs (-īs)	mare	-ia	genus	-a	flūmen	-a
Abl.	lūce	-ibus	mīlite	-ibus	nāve	-ibus	nocte	-ibus	marī	-ibus	genere	-ibus	flūmine	-ibus

[1]Nouns ending in **-is** or **-es** that have the same number of syllables in the genitive and the nominative take **-ium** in the genitive plural and, sometimes, **-īs** in the accusative plural.

Nouns whose bases end in double consonants take **-ium** in the genitive plural and, sometimes, **-īs** in the accusative plural.

Neuter nouns ending in **-e, -al,** or **-ar** take **-ī** in the ablative singular, **-ia** in the nominative and accusative plural, and **-ium** in the genitive plural.

Irregular Nouns of the Third Declension

A. Bōs, bovis (ox, cow) has **boum** in the genitive plural and **bōbus** or **būbus** in the dative and ablative plural.
B. Carō, carnis (flesh), fem., has **carnium** in the genitive plural.
C. Vīs (force in sing., strength in plur.), fem., is declined **vīs, vis, vī, vim, vī, (plur.) vīrēs, vīrium, vīribus, vīrēs (-īs), vīribus.**
D. Turris, turris (tower), fem., and sitis, sitis (thirst), fem., have **-im** in the accusative singular, and **-ī** in the ablative singular.
E. Senex, senis (old man), masc., has **senum** in the genitive plural.

F. Sus, suis (swine), masc. and fem., has **suum** in the genitive plural, and **subus** (suibus) in the dative and ablative plural.
G. The declension of Iuppiter (Jupiter): **Iuppiter, Iovis, Iovī, Iovem, Iove.**
H. Iter, itineris (route, march, journey), neuter.
I. Hērōs, hērōis, hērōī, hērōa, hērōe is a Greek masc. noun meaning hero.
J. Ilias, Iliados (The Iliad), fem., is declined like hērōs.

Fourth Declension Nouns

Most fourth declension nouns are masculine and are formed from the 4th principal part of the verb. Feminine nouns of the 4th declension are: anus (old woman), **manus** (hand), **domus** (house), **tribus** (tribe). There are also a few names of trees, such as **pinus** (pine) and **ficus** (fig). There are very few neuters in the 4th declension; **cornū** (horn) and **pecū** (cattle) are two. The ending **-ubus** sometimes replaces **-ibus** in the dative and ablative plural; tribus and lacus (lake) are common examples.

	Masc. (port)		Fem. (house)		Neut. (knee)	
	Sing.	Plur.	Sing.	Plur.	Sing.	Plur.
Nom.	portus	-ūs	domus	-ūs	genū	-ua
Gen.	portūs	-uum	domūs (-ī)	-uum (-ōrum)	genūs	-uum
Dat.	portuī (-ū)	-ibus	domuī (-ō)	-ibus	genū	-ibus
Acc.	portum	-ūs	domum	-ōs (-ūs)	genū	-ua
Abl.	portū	-ibus	domō (-ū)	-ibus	genū	-ibus

Note: Domus has forms in both 2nd and 4th declensions.

Fifth Declension Nouns

Only 3 nouns in the 5th declension are declined throughout: **diēs, rēs,** and **merīdiēs** (noon, south).
The following are used in the singular throughout, but only in the nominative and the accusative plural: **aciēs** (sharp edge, line of battle), **effigiēs** (likeness), **faciēs** (face), **glaciēs** (ice), **seriēs** (series, succession), **speciēs** (appearance), and **spēs** (hope).

All 5th declension nouns are feminine except diēs, which is occasionally feminine, and merīdiēs, which is masculine.

	Sing.	Plur.	Sing.	Plur.
Nom.	diēs (day)	diēs	rēs (matter)	rēs
Gen.	diēī	-ērum	reī	rērum
Dat.	diēī	-ēbus	reī	rēbus
Acc.	diem	-ēs	rem	rēs
Abl.	diē	-ēbus	rē	rēbus

Defective Nouns

Many Latin nouns are defective in case. Outstanding are nouns having only two cases: **fors**, nominative (chance), **forte**, ablative (by chance); and **spontis**, genitive (accord), **sponte**, ablative (of one's accord). Other nouns are defective in number. These nouns are used only in the plural: **arma, armōrum,** neut.

(arms); **castra, castrōrum,** neut. (camp); **Kalendae, Kalendārum,** fem. (The Kalends); **īnsidiae, īnsidiārum,** fem. (ambush); **īnferī, -ōrum,** masc. (the dead, the underworld).

5. ADJECTIVES
First and Second Declension Adjectives

Adjectives agree with their nouns in gender, number, and case. Those in the predicate after **sum** (be) agree with the subject, as in English. Most masculine adjectives are declined like ager, puer, or dominus, neuter adjectives like caelum, and feminine adjectives like terra.

	Masculine		Feminine		Neuter	
	Sing.	Plur.	Sing.	Plur.	Sing.	Plur.
Nom.	bonus	-ī	bona	-ae	bonum	-a
Gen.	bonī	-ōrum	bonae	-ārum	bonī	-ōrum
Dat.	bonō	-īs	bonae	-īs	bonō	-īs
Acc.	bonum	-ōs	bonam	-ās	bonum	-a
Abl.	bonō	-īs	bonā	-īs	bonō	-īs

Third Declension Adjectives

Third declension adjectives fall into four distinct categories: (1) *three-termination,* with separate endings for all three genders, like **ācer;** (2) *two-termination,* with the same endings for masculine and feminine, like **omnis;** (3) *one-termination,* with the nominative singular the same in all genders, like **potēns;** and (4) the *comparative* of all adjectives, like **longior.** Present participles are declined like **potēns.**

(1) ācer *(keen)*

	Masc.		Fem.		Neut.	
	Sing.	*Plur.*	*Sing.*	*Plur.*	*Sing.*	*Plur.*
Nom.	ācer	ācrēs	ācris	ācrēs	ācre	ācria
Gen.	ācris	-ium	ācris	-ium	ācris	-ium
Dat.	ācrī	-ibus	ācrī	-ibus	ācrī	-ibus
Acc.	ācrem	-ēs (-īs)	ācrem	-ēs (-īs)	ācre	-ia
Abl.	ācrī	-ibus	ācrī	-ibus	ācrī	-ibus

(2) omnis *(all)*

	Masc. & Fem.		Neut.	
	Sing.	*Plur.*	*Sing.*	*Plur.*
Nom.	omnis	-ēs	omne	-ia
Gen.	omnis	-ium	omnis	-ium
Dat.	omnī	-ibus	omnī	-ibus
Acc.	omnem	-ēs (-īs)	omne	-ia
Abl.	omnī	-ibus	omnī	-ibus

(3) potēns *(powerful)*

	Masc. & Fem.		Neut.	
	Sing.	*Plur.*	*Sing.*	*Plur.*
Nom.	potēns	potentēs	potēns	potentia
Gen.	potentis	-ium	potentis	-ium
Dat.	potentī	-ibus	potentī	-ibus
Acc.	potentem	-ēs (-īs)	potēns	-ia
Abl.	potentī (-e)	-ibus	potentī (-e)	-ibus

(4) longior *(longer)*

	Masc. & Fem.		Neut.	
	Sing.	*Plur.*	*Sing.*	*Plur.*
Nom.	longior	longiōrēs	longius	longiōra
Gen.	longiōris	-um	longiōris	-um
Dat.	longiōrī	-ibus	longiōrī	-ibus
Acc.	longiōrem	-ēs (-īs)	longius	-a
Abl.	longiōre	-ibus	longiōre	-ibus

(5) plūs *(more)*

	Masc. & Fem.	Neut.	
	Plur.	*Sing.*	*Plur.*
Nom.	plūrēs	plūs	plūra
Gen.	-ium	plūris	-ium
Dat.	-ibus	plūrī	-ibus
Acc.	-ēs (-īs)	plūs	-a
Abl.	-ibus	plūre	-ibus

The Nine Irregular Adjectives

There are nine adjectives ("the naughty nine") which are regular in the plural and irregular in the singular. The plurals of these words are declined like **bonus.** With the exceptions noted, the *singulars* of these adjectives are declined like **tōtus.**

alius *other, another*
(neut. — aliud)
ūllus *any*
ūnus *one, alone*
neuter *neither*
(gen. — neutrīus)

alter *the other*
(gen. — alterīus)
nūllus *no, none*
sōlus *alone, only*
uter *which of two*
(gen. — utrīus)

tōtus *(whole, all)*

	Masc.	Fem.	Neut.
Nom.	tōtus	tōta	tōtum
Gen.	tōtīus	tōtīus	tōtīus
Dat.	tōtī	tōtī	tōtī
Acc.	tōtum	tōtam	tōtum
Abl.	tōtō	tōtā	tōtō

Comparison of Adjectives

There are three degrees of comparison in Latin, just as there are in English: *positive, comparative,* and *superlative.* The *comparative* is formed by adding **-ior** for the masculine and feminine, and **-ius** for the neuter to the base of the *positive.* The *superlative* is formed by adding **-issimus, -a, -um** to the base. The *comparative* is declined like **longior** on page 6 of this chart; the *positive* is declined like bonus for 1st and 2nd declension, like omnis for third declension adjectives. The *superlative* is declined like bonus.

Note: Six adjectives ending in **-lis** (facilis, difficilis, similis, dissimilis, gracilis, humilis) add **-limus** instead of -issimus to the base to form the *superlative.* (facilis, facilior, facillimus.)

Note: Adjectives ending in **-er** add **-rimus** instead of -issimus to form the *superlative.*

miser, -a, -um   miserior, miserius   miserrimus, -a, -um
ācer, -is, -e   ācrior, ācrius   ācerrimus, -a, -um

Note: Adjectives ending in -ius or -eus add **magis** to form the comparative and **maximē** to form the superlative: idōneus, magis idōneus, maximē idōneus.

REGULAR FORMS

Positive	Comparative	Superlative
longus, -a, -um	longior, longius	longissimus, -a, -um
fortis, forte	fortior, fortius	fortissimus, -a, -um

IRREGULAR COMPARISONS

Positive	Comparative	Superlative
bonus *(good)*	melior	optimus
malus *(bad)*	peior	pessimus
magnus *(large)*	maior	maximus
multus *(much)*	plūs	plūrimus
multī *(many)*	plūrēs	plūrimī
parvus *(small)*	minor	minimus
maledicus *(slanderous)*	maledicentior	maledicentissimus
malevolus *(spiteful)*	malevolentior	malevolentissimus

6. PRONOUNS

Pronouns, as the name implies, take the place of nouns. At times, they are used as adjectives, to modify nouns. Under those circumstances, they agree with the nouns in gender, number, and case.

Personal Pronouns

	1st Person				2nd Person			
	Sing.		*Plur.*		*Sing.*		*Plur.*	
Nom.	ego	*I*	nōs	*we*	tū	*you*	vōs	*you*
Gen.	meī	*of me*	nostrum, nostrī	*of us*	tuī	*of you*	vestrum, vestrī	*of you*
Dat.	mihi	*to me*	nōbīs	*to us*	tibi	*to you*	vōbīs	*to you*
Acc.	mē	*me*	nōs	*us*	tē	*you*	vōs	*you*
Abl.	mē	*by,* etc., *me*	nōbīs	*by,* etc., *us*	tē	*by,* etc., *you*	vōbīs	*by,* etc., *you*

3rd Person: A demonstrative pronoun is used as the pronoun of the 3rd person.

The Demonstrative Pronouns (or Adjectives)

There are 5 demonstratives used to point out special objects or persons.
Hic *(this here)* refers to what is near the speaker in place, time, or thought. Sometimes the word may also mean *he, she,* or *it.*
Ille *(that there)* refers to something remote from the speaker. It also means *that famous.*
Is, ea, id are most commonly used for *he, she,* or *it.* They may also mean *this* or *that.*
Iste *(that — nearby* or *that of yours)* is often used comtemptuously.
Īdem means *the same.*

Masc.	Fem.	Neut.	Masc.	Fem.	Neut.
hic	haec	hoc	ille	illa	illud
huius	huius	huius	illīus	illīus	illīus
huic	huic	huic	illī	illī	illī
hunc	hanc	hoc	illum	illam	illud
hōc	hāc	hōc	illō	illā	illō
hī	hae	haec	illī	illae	illa
hōrum	hārum	hōrum	illōrum	illārum	illōrum
hīs	hīs	hīs	illīs	illīs	illīs
hōs	hās	haec	illōs	illās	illa
hīs	hīs	hīs	illīs	illīs	illīs

Masc.	Fem.	Neut.	Masc.	Fem.	Neut.
is	ea	id	iste	ista	istud
ēius	ēius	ēius	istīus	istīus	istīus
eī	eī	eī	istī	istī	istī
eum	eam	id	istum	istam	istud
eō	eā	eō	istō	istā	istō
eī	eae	ea	istī	istae	ista
eōrum	eārum	eōrum	istōrum	istārum	istōrum
eīs	eīs	eīs	istīs	istīs	istīs
eōs	eās	ea	istōs	istās	ista
eīs	eīs	eīs	istīs	istīs	istīs

Masc.	Fem.	Neut.
īdem	eadem	idem
ēiusdem	ēiusdem	ēiusdem
eīdem	eīdem	eīdem
eundem	eandem	idem
eōdem	eādem	eōdem
eīdem	eaedem	eadem
eōrundem	eārundem	eōrundem
eīsdem	eīsdem	eīsdem
eōsdem	eāsdem	eadem
eīsdem	eīsdem	eīsdem

Indefinite Pronouns

Quis, quispiam, aliquis, and **quīdam** are the indefinite pronouns. **Quis** is usually used immediately after **sī, nisi, nē,** and **num.** Only the quis and quī of the indefinites may be declined. **quis** is declined like the interrogative below; **quī** is declined like the relative.

Interrogative Pronouns

The interrogative pronoun, as its name implies, introduces a question. **Quis** means *who,* and **quid** means *what.* Declension is like the relative, **quis** for **quī, quid** for **quod,** with the plural declined the same.

Possessive Pronouns (or Adjectives)

1st Person Sing.
meus, -a, -um *my, mine*
(Declined like bonus)

1st Person Plur.
noster, nostra, nostrum
(Declined like pulcher)

2nd Person Sing.
tuus, tua, tuum *your*

2nd Person Plur.
vester, vestra, vestrum

3rd Person Reflexive Possessive
suus, sua, suum *his, her, its, their*

Suus refers to the subject and agrees with the noun modified in gender, number, and case.

Reflexive Pronouns

The reflexive pronoun of the third person has a single declension for singular and plural, and all three genders.

Nom.	(none)	*Note:* The oblique cases of the
Gen.	suī	1st and 2nd person of the *per-*
Dat.	sibi	*sonal* pronouns are used ref-
Acc.	sē	lexively.
Abl.	sē	amō mē. *(I love myself.)*

The Intensive Pronoun Ipse

Ipse is used to emphasize nouns and pronouns of any person and agrees with the pronoun contained in the verb. Lēgātus **ipse** haec dīxit. *The envoy himself said these things.*

	Sing.			*Plur.*		
ipse	ipsa	ipsum	ipsī	ipsae	ipsa
ipsīus	ipsīus	ipsīus	ipsōrum	ipsārum	ipsōrum
ipsī	ipsī	ipsī	ipsīs	ipsīs	ipsīs
ipsum	ipsam	ipsum	ipsōs	ipsās	ipsa
ipsō	ipsā	ipsō	ipsīs	ipsīs	ipsīs

Relative Pronouns

Quī, quae, quod *(who, which)* is the most commonly used of the relative pronouns (or adjectives).

	Sing.			*Plur.*		
Masc.	*Fem.*	*Neut.*	*Masc.*	*Fem.*	*Neut.*
quī	quae	quod	quī	quae	quae
cūius	cūius	cūius	quōrum	quārum	quōrum
cui	cui	cui	quibus	quibus	quibus
quem	quam	quod	quōs	quās	quae
quō	quā	quō	quibus	quibus	quibus

Nominative Case

1. The subject of a finite verb is nominative. **Caesar** veniet. *Caesar will come.*
2. Predicate Nominative (Subject Complement). After the verb *to be* or any form thereof the subject complement replaces an object of the verb. It is in the same case as the subject. Herculēs **fīlius** Alcmēnae erat. *Hercules was the son of Alcmena.*

Vocative Case

1. The vocative case is used for direct address. Its forms are exactly like those of the nominative case, except for 2nd declension nouns ending in -us or -ius. Et tū, **Brūte!** *You, too, Brutus!* **Mī fīlī!** *My son!*

Genitive Case

1. Possession: Equus **Caesaris**. *Caesar's horse.* BUT: Equus **meus**... *My horse...* (Possessive adjective)
2. Quality (When a noun is modified): Vir **magnae virtūtis**... *A man of great courage.*
3. Subjective: Adventus **Caesaris**... *The arrival of Caesar.* (If the noun "arrival" were changed to a verb, *Caesar* would become the subject of it.)
4. Objective: Amor **pecūniae**... *The love of money*... (If the noun "love" were changed to a verb, *money* would be the object of it.)
   Note: These are nouns of action, agency, and feeling.
5. Partitive: Nihil **vīnī**... *No wine...* (*Nothing of wine*), Pars **exercitūs**... *Part of the army...*
   Note: The following adjectives modify their noun directly and are not followed by the genitive:
   omnis — *all of* summus — *top of*
   tōtus — *whole of* medius — *middle of*
   Cardinal numerals and quīdam take ex or dē plus the ablative case rather than the partitive genitive.
6. A possessive, partitive, or genitive of quality may stand in the predicate of a sentence. Hic gladius est **Caesaris**. *This sword is Caesar's.*
7. With verbs of remembering and forgetting. Ipse **mātris suae** meminerat. *He remembered (was mindful of) his mother.*
   Note: To remember or forget a *thing* is rendered by meminī plus the accusative case. **Omnia** meminit. *He remembers everything.*
8. Verbs of reminding take the accusative of the person and the genitive of the thing. Cicerō Catilīnam **facinōrum** admonēbat. *Cicero was warning Catiline of his crimes.*
9. Verbs of accusing or condemning take the genitive. Mē **inertiae** damnat. *He condemns me for laziness.*
10. With miseret, paenitet, piget, pudet, and taedet, the genitive is used as the cause of the feeling. Mē paenitet **inimīcitiae**. *I am sorry for my unfriendliness.*
11. Interest (*it is to the interest of*) and refert (*it interests*) take the genitive of the person. **Cicerōnis** intererat Clōdium morī. *It was to Cicero's interest for Clodius to die.*
12. With potior, sometimes the genitive is used instead of the usual ablative. **Oppidī** potītus est. *He took possession of the town.*
13. Preceding causā and gratiā (*for the sake of*) a gerund in the genitive or a noun modified by a gerundive, both genitive, is often used to express purpose. **Pugnāndī** causā, *in order to fight;* **urbis expugnāndae** causā, *in order to capture the city.*
14. Genitive of indefinite value is expressed by tantī (*of such value*), quantī (*of how great value*), magnī (*of great value*), parvī (*of little value*), and their comparative or superlative genitive forms. Est mihi **tantī**. *It is worthwhile (it is of such value) to me.*

Dative Case

1. Indirect object: **Fīliō** fābulam nārrāvit. *He told his son a story.*
2. Indirect object with an intransitive verb. Crēdite **mihi**. *Believe me.*
   Tibi persuādēbō ut discēdās. *I shall persuade you to go away.*
   Note: When these verbs are in the passive, the indirect object is retained, and the verbs become impersonal. **Tibi** persuādēbitur ut discēdās. *You will be persuaded to leave.*
3. Indirect Object with Compounds. Some verbs compounded with ad, ante, con, in, ob, post, prae, prō, sub, super in such a way as to change their meanings call for a dative object. Caesar Brūtum **exercituī** praefēcit. *Caesar put Brutus in charge of the army.*
4. Dative of Possession (with the verb *to be*). **Imperātōrī** est gladius. *The emperor has a sword.*
5. Dative of agent is used with the gerundive and some of the perfect passive constructions to show the "doer" of the action. Oppidum **Caesarī** est oppugnandum. *The town ought to be besieged by Caesar.* **Mihi** dēlīberātum est. *I have deliberated.*
6. Dative of Purpose. Vēnit **auxiliō** castrīs. *He came as an aid to the camp.* The following words are most commonly used with this construction:
   auxilium - *aid,* praesidium - *guard,*
   cūra - *care,* subsidium - *reserve*
7. Dative of Reference. The person or thing affected in the sentence ...**quibus** locus parātur ...*for whom a place is being made ready.*
   Note: When the datives of purpose and reference are used together, they are called the double dative. Flūmen erat **magnō impedīmentō Gallīs**. *The river was a great hindrance to the Gauls.*
8. Dative of Separation. Occasionally, after compounds with ab, dē, ex, ad, the dative occurs instead of the usual ablative. Hunc timōrem **mihi** ēripe. *Take this fear from me.*
9. The dative occurs with adjectives of *fitness* (aptus), *nearness* (proximus), *likeness* (similis), *friendliness* (amīcus), and their opposites. Gallī sunt proximī **Germānīs**. *The Gauls are near the Germans.*

Accusative Case

1. Direct Object of a transitive verb. Brūtus **Caesarem** vulnerāvit. *Brutus wounded Caesar.*
2. Subject of the infinitive. In indirect statements and after iubeō (*order*), patior (*allow*), and sinō (*permit*), the subject of the infinitive goes into the accusative case. Dīxit **ducem** fūgisse. *He said that the leader had fled.*
3. Predicate accusative or object complement where a second accusative is used after appellō (*name*), dēligō (*choose*), creō (*make*). Pompeium **cōnsulem** creāvērunt. *They elected Pompey consul.*
4. After verbs of asking and teaching, two accusatives are found: one of the direct object, the other the things asked or taught. **Mē sententiam** rogāvit. *He asked me my opinion.*
5. Time how long. **Multās hōrās** pugnāvērunt. *They fought for many hours.*
6. Extent of Space. **Multa mīlia** passuum iter fēcērunt. *They marched many miles.*
7. Object of certain prepositions. These prepositions take an accusative object: ad, ante, circum, contrā, inter, intrā, ob, per, post, prope, propter, super, trāns, ultrā. Per **hōs annōs**... *During these years...*
8. Ad with the accusative gerund or a noun modified by the gerundive, both accusative, is often used to express purpose. Ad **pugnandam,** *in order to fight;* ad **urbem expugnandam,** *in order to capture the city.*

Ablative Case

1. Object of certain Prepositions (all those not listed as governing the accusative case). The more common ones are: ā/ab, cum, dē, ē/ex, in, prae, prō, sine, sub.
2. Personal agent, expressed with a passive verb and a person, with ā/ab. Caesar ā **Brūtō** interfectus est. *Caesar was killed by Brutus.*
3. Separation. With a verb of motion, the ablative is always used. Hostēs ā **fīnibus** prohibent. *They keep the enemy from their territory.*
4. Place from which. Ex **urbe** ēgressus est. *He left the city.*
5. Ablative of Cause. **Timōre** commōtus est. *He was frightened (moved by fear).*
6. Ablative of Means. With the deponent verbs ūtor (*use*), fruor (*enjoy*), fungor (*accomplish*), potior (*gain*), and vēscor (*feed on*), the ablative is usually used. **Gladiīs** ūsus est. *He used swords.*
7. With opus and usus (meaning *need*). Opus est **armīs**. *There is need of arms.*
8. Ablative of accordance. **Suā sponte**... *Of his own accord...* **Nostrīs mōribus**... *According to our customs...*
9. Ablative of place where (with in only). If in is omitted with names of towns, domus, rūs, and humus, the locative case is used (see below). In **urbe** est. *He is in the city.*
10. Ablative of Comparison. When quam (*than*) is omitted in comparisons, the ablative is used. Mare est altius **flūmine**. *The sea is deeper than the river.*
11. Specification. This ablative tells in what respect something is done or is true. Mōns magnus **altitūdine**... *A mountain great in height...*
12. Degree of Difference. After comparatives, this ablative shows the extent or degree to which the objects differ. Puer est altior quam puella **ūnō pede**. *The boy is taller than the girl by a foot.*
13. Ablative of manner, telling "how," may omit the usual cum if the noun is modified. **Magnā** (cum) **celeritāte** fūgērunt. *They fled with great speed.*
14. Accompaniment (regularly with cum). Cum **coniugibus**... *With wives...*
15. Ablative of means or instrument of an action occurs without a preposition in most cases. Mīlitēs **gladiīs** vulnerātī erant. *The soldiers had been wounded by swords.*
16. Ablative of time when, without a preposition. **Prīmō annō**... *In the first year...*
17. Ablative Absolute. This construction consists of a noun or pronoun in the ablative case plus a present active or perfect passive participle, or two nouns in the ablative case, or a noun and an adjective, with the participle understood. The construction is usually translated by a clause referring to time (*when*), cause (*since, because*), concession (*although*), condition (*if*). In any given instance any of the above translations may be appropriate, depending upon the sense of the rest of the context. **Mīlitibus** vulnerātīs, dux fūgit. *When the soldiers were wounded the leader fled.* (This could also be: *Because the soldiers...*)
18. Quality or Description. Vir **magnā virtūte**... *A man of great courage...*

Locative Case

The locative case is used only to indicate "place where" or "place at which" with names of towns or cities, humus (*soil*), domus (*home*), and rūs (*the country*). In all other cases the ablative of "place where" with the preposition in is used. The locative endings are:

	Sing.	Plur.
1st Declension	-ae	-īs
2nd Declension	-ī	-īs
3rd Declension	-ī or -e	-ibus

Rōmae — *in Rome,* domī — *at home,* rūrī — *in the country*

8. NUMERALS

Of the numerals, only ūnus, duo, trēs, the hundreds, and the plural of mīlle are declined.

	ŪNUS			DUO			TRĒS		MĪLLE
	M.	F.	N.	M.	F.	N.	M. & F.	N.	P. only
Nom.	ūnus	ūna	ūnum	duo	duae	duo	trēs	tria	mīlia
Gen.	ūnīus	ūnīus	ūnīus	duōrum	duārum	duōrum	trium	trium	mīlium
Dat.	ūnī	ūnī	ūnī	duōbus	duābus	duōbus	tribus	tribus	mīlibus
Acc.	ūnum	ūnam	ūnum	duōs	duās	duo	trēs (-īs)	tria	mīlia
Abl.	ūnō	ūnā	ūnō	duōbus	duābus	duōbus	tribus	tribus	mīlibus

There are four types of numerals: Cardinal Numerals (adjectives) one, two, etc.; Ordinal Numerals (adjectives) first, second, etc.; Distributives (adjectives) one by one, two by two, three each, etc.; Numerical Adverbs (once, twice, etc.).

	Cardinals	Ordinals	Distributives	Adverbs	Numerals
1	ūnus, -a, -um	prīmus, -a, -um	singulī, -ae, -a	semel	I
2	duo, duae, duo	secundus	bīnī	bis	II
3	trēs, tria	tertius	ternī (trinī)	ter	III
4	quattuor	quārtus	quaternī	quater	IV
5	quīnque	quīntus	quīnī	quīnquiēns	V
6	sex	sextus	sēnī	sexiēns	VI
7	septem	septimus	septēnī	septiēns	VII
8	octō	octāvus	octōnī	octiēns	VIII
9	novem	nōnus	novēnī	noviēns	IX
10	decem	decimus	dēnī	deciēns	X
11	ūndecim	ūndecimus	ūndēnī	ūndeciēns	XI
12	duodecim	duodecimus	duodēnī	duodeciēns	XII
13	tredecim	tertius decimus	ternī dēnī	terdeciēns	XIII
14	quattuordecim	quārtus decimus	quaternī dēnī	quater deciēns	XIV
15	quīndecim	quīntus decimus	quīnī dēnī	quīndeciēns	XV
16	sēdecim	sextus decimus	sēnī dēnī	sēdeciēns	XVI
17	septendecim	septimus decimus	septēnī dēnī	septiēns deciēns	XVII
18	duodēvīgintī (octōdecim)	duodēvīcēsimus (octāvus decimus)	duodēvīcēnī (octōnī dēnī)	duodēvīciēns (octiēns deciēns)	XVIII
19	ūndēvīgintī (novendecim)	ūndēvīcēsimus (nōnus decimus)	ūndēvīcēnī (novēnī dēnī)	ūndēvīciēns (noviēns deciēns)	XIX
20	vīgintī	vīcēsimus	vīcēnī	vīciēns	XX
21	vīgintī ūnus	ūnus et vīcēsimus	vīcēnī singulī	vīciēns semel	XXI
30	trīgintā	trīcēsimus	trīcēnī	trīciēns	XXX
40	quadrāgintā	quadrāgēsimus	quadrāgēnī	quadrāgiēns	XL
50	quīnquāgintā	quīnquāgēsimus	quīnquāgēnī	quīnquāgiēns	L
60	sexāgintā	sexāgēsimus	sexāgēnī	sexāgiēns	LX
70	septuāgintā	septuāgēsimus	septuāgēnī	septuāgiēns	LXX
80	octōgintā	octōgēsimus	octōgēnī	octōgiēns	LXXX
90	nōnāgintā	nōnāgēsimus	nōnāgēnī	nōnāgiēns	XC
100	centum	centēsimus	centēnī	centiēns	C
101	centum ūnus	centēsimus prīmus	centēnī singulī	centiēns semel	CI
200	ducentī, -ae, -a	duocentēsimus	ducēnī	ducentiēns	CC
300	trecentī	trecentēsimus	trecēnī	trecentiēns	CCC
400	quadringentī	quādringentēsimus	quadringēnī	quadringentiēns	CCCC
500	quīngentī	quīngentēsimus	quīngēnī	quīngentiēns	D
1000	mīlle	mīllēsimus	mīllenī	mīlliēns	M
2000	duo mīlia	bis mīllēsimus	bīna mīlia	bis mīlliēns	MM

9. PREPOSITIONS, PREFIXES

Most of the prepositions in Latin are used to govern the use of the accusative case. About one third of them govern the ablative, and a few govern both cases, depending upon the verb used in the sentence (see Syntax of Verbs, page 4). Many prepositions are also commonly used as prefixes. Attached to the front of a word, they give it a different shade of meaning. Examples are below.

Preposition	Case	Meaning	Derivative	Meaning
ā, ab	Ablative	*away from*	**ab**dūcō	*lead away*
ad	Accusative	*to*	**ad**dūcō	*lead to, influence*
ante	Accusative	*before*	**ante**cēdō	*go before*
apud	Accusative	*at, among*		
circum	Accusative	*around, about*	**circum**ferō	*carry around*
contrā	Accusative	*against*	**contrā**dīcō	*speak against*
cum, con, com	Ablative	*with*	**con**trahō	*draw together*
dē	Ablative	*down from*	**dē**scendō	*climb down*
ē, ex	Ablative	*out from*	**ex**pellō	*drive out*
in	Accusative	*into*	**in**iciō	*hurl into*
in	Ablative	*in (place where)*		
inter	Accusative	*between, among*	**inter**mittō	*interrupt*
ob	Accusative	*on account of*	**oc**currō	*run to meet*
per	Accusative	*through*	**per**rumpō	*break through*
post	Accusative	*after*	**post**pōnō	*put after*
prae	Ablative	*in front of*	**prae**ficiō	*put in command*
praeter	Accusative	*along by, past*	**praeter**eō	*go past*
prō	Ablative	*in front of*	**prō**fundō	*pour forth*
propter	Accusative	*on account of*	**propter**eā	*on that account*
re-, red-	Prefix only	*back*	**re**dimō	*buy back*
sub	Accusative	*up from under*	**sub**vertō	*upset*
sub	Ablative	*under*	**sub**trahō	*draw from under*
super	Accusative	*above*	**super**gredior	*step over*
trāns	Accusative	*across*	**trāns**eō	*go across*
ultrā	Accusative	*beyond*	**ultrā**mundānus	*out of this world*

10. FORMATION AND COMPARISON OF ADVERBS

Positive adverbs are formed regularly by adding **-ē** to the base of adjectives of the 1st and 2nd declensions (longē). Adjectives of the 3rd declension may be changed to adverbs by adding **-iter** to the base (fortiter). Those with a base of **-nt** simply add **-er** (prūdenter). Examples are below.

Positive	Comparative	Superlative
longē	longius	longissimē
fortiter	fortius	fortissimē
miserē	miserius	miserrimē
ācriter	ācrius	ācerrimē
facile	facilius	facillimē
prūdenter	prūdentius	prūdentissimē
bene	melius	optimē
male	pēius	pessimē
magnopere	magis	maximē
multum	plūs	plūrimum
parum	minus	minimē
diū	diūtius	diūtissimē

Adverbs of Location

hīc *(here)*	hinc *(hence)*	hūc *(hither)*
ibi *(there)*	inde *(thence)*	eō *(thither)*
illīc *(there)*	illinc *(thence)*	illūc *(thither)*
istīc *(there)*	istinc *(thence)*	istūc *(thither)*
ubi *(where)*	unde *(whence)*	quō *(whither)*

hāc *(by this way)*	usquam *(anywhere)*
eā *(by that way)*	nusquam *(nowhere)*
illā *(by that way)*	intrō *(inwardly, from the outside in)*
istā *(by that way)*	
quā *(by what way)*	extrō *(outwardly, from the inside out)*
ultrō *(beyond)*	

Adverbs of Time

prīmum *(first)*	iam *(already)*
deinde *(next)*	iam diū *(long ago)*
semper *(always)*	iam nōn *(no longer)*
umquam *(ever)*	prīdiē *(the day before)*
numquam *(never)*	saepe *(often)*
cum *(when)*	hodiē *(today)*
ut *(when)*	cotīdiē *(daily)*
quandō *(when?)*	herī *(yesterday)*
mox *(soon)*	crās *(tomorrow)*
dum *(while)*	nōndum *(not yet)*

Interrogative Adverbs

-ne, an enclitic, expects the answer *"maybe."*
Ēnumerābis**ne** puerōs? *(Will you count the boys?)*
Nōnne expects the answer *"yes."*
Nōnne ībis? *(You will go, won't you?)*
Num expects the answer *"no."*
Num manēbis? *(You won't stay, will you?)*
An, -ne, anne, utrum, num, introducing indirect questions, all mean *"whether."*
Nesciō utrum veniam **an** eam. *(I don't know whether I'm coming or going.)*

Negative Adverbs (Particles)

nōn *(not)*, nē, in a prohibition *(not)*
haud *(not)*, nē, in a purpose clause *(lest)*
minimē *(not at all)*, nē, after verb of fearing *(that)*
nec, neque *(and not)* nēve, neu *(and not)*
neque...neque, nec...nec *(neither...nor)*
nē...quidem, with the emphasized word between *(not even)*
nōn sōlum...sed etiam *(not only...but also)*
nē quis, nē quid *(so that no one, so that nothing)*

Relative Adverbs

Relative adverbs introduce certain clauses:
ubi *(where)* Nesciō **ubi** puer sit. *(I don't know where the boy is.)*
quō *(whither)* cognōvī **quō** fūgisset. *(I learned whither he had fled.)*
unde *(whence)*
cum *(when, since, although)*
quārē *(why)*

Adverbs of Degree

quam *(how)*	ergō, itaque, igitur *(therefore)*
tam *(so)*	proptereā *(on this account)*
paene *(almost)*	ita, sīc *(thus, so)*
ut, utī *(how)*	cūr, quārē *(why)*

Card Storagebox Bottom (1 of 2)

A fold	fold	fold **A**
cut	fold	cut

glue A here

B

fold

glue A here

Assembly Instructions

This is the inside of the box.

1. Cut out the pattern following the outside lines.

2. Cut along the solid lines between the A tabs and B sides.

3. Prefold the box along all of the dashed lines.

4. Glue the A tabs to the inside of the B sides. Alternately you may tape the tabs down, and apply additional tape to the outside corners to hold the box together.

BOX BOTTOM

glue A here

B

fold

glue A here

cut	fold	cut
A fold		fold **A**

Vergil Vocabulary Cards for AP* Selections

Bonus: Graphic Latin Grammar Cards
by Dennis De Young

587 vocabulary cards from the AP* Selections of Vergil's *Aeneid*. All vocabulary occurring five or more times is included on the cards. Cards are bound into book form and printed on perforated cardstock, with easily assembled storage boxes. Bonus removable full-page cards for quick reference while reading: Full AP* selections vocabulary list • *Graphic Latin Grammar* • Meter • Rhetorical Terms, Figures of Speech, and Rhetorical Devices.

ISBN 0-86516-610-2

A

fold

fold

A

cut

fold

cut

glue A here

B

fold

fold

B

glue A here

Assembly Instructions

This is the inside of the box.

1. Cut out the pattern following the outside lines.

2. Cut along the solid lines between the A tabs and B sides.

3. Prefold the box along all of the dashed lines.

4. Glue the A tabs to the inside of the B sides. Alternately you may tape the tabs down, and apply additional tape to the outside corners to hold the box together.

BOX BOTTOM

glue A here

glue A here

cut

fold

cut

A

fold

fold

A

Vergil Vocabulary Cards for AP* Selections

Bonus: Graphic Latin Grammar Cards

by Dennis De Young

587 vocabulary cards from the AP* Selections of Vergil's *Aeneid*. All vocabulary occurring five or more times is included on the cards. Cards are bound into book form and printed on perforated cardstock, with easily assembled storage boxes. Bonus removable full-page cards for quick reference while reading: Full AP* selections vocabulary list • *Graphic Latin Grammar* • Meter • Rhetorical Terms, Figures of Speech, and Rhetorical Devices.

ISBN 0-86516-610-2

A

fold

fold

A

cut

fold

cut

glue
A
here

glue
A
here

Assembly Instructions

This is the inside of the box.

1. Cut out the pattern following the outside lines.

2. Cut along the solid lines between the A tabs and B sides.

3. Prefold the box along all of the dashed lines.

4. Glue the A tabs to the inside of the B sides. Alternately you may tape the tabs down, and apply additional tape to the outside corners to hold the box together.

B

fold

fold

B

glue
A
here

glue
A
here

BOX TOP

cut

fold

cut

A

fold

fold

A

ISBN: 0-86516-610-2

VERGIL
VOCABULARY CARDS
for AP Selections*

DENNIS DE YOUNG

Bolchazy-Carducci Publishers, Inc.
1000 Brown St., Unit 101, Wauconda, IL 60084
Phone: (847) 526-4344; *Fax:* (847) 526-2867
www.bolchazy.com

Card Storagebox Top (2 of 2)

A

fold

fold

A

cut

fold

cut

glue
A
here

glue
A
here

B

fold

Assembly Instructions

This is the inside of the box.

1. Cut out the pattern following the outside lines.

2. Cut along the solid lines between the A tabs and B sides.

3. Prefold the box along all of the dashed lines.

4. Glue the A tabs to the inside of the B sides. Alternately you may tape the tabs down, and apply additional tape to the outside corners to hold the box together.

fold

B

glue
A
here

BOX TOP

glue
A
here

cut

fold

cut

A

fold

fold

A

ISBN: 0-86516-610-2

VERGIL
VOCABULARY CARDS
for AP Selections*

VERGIL VOCABULARY CARDS
for AP* Selections

VERGIL VOCABULARY CARDS
for AP* Selections

DENNIS DE YOUNG

**Bolchazy-Carducci
Publishers, Inc.**
1000 Brown St., Unit 101, Wauconda, IL 60084
Phone: (847) 526-4344; *Fax:* (847) 526-2867
www.bolchazy.com